THOUGHTS & TANGENTS

Shane Keenan

Thoughts and tangents of a 21st century man

Table of Contents

Value & Purpose

The purpose is what a thing is supposed to do. A book is supposed to be read, a chair to be sat on. The value is attributed to it based on how well it fulfils this purpose. A valueless cup is one full of holes, one that does not achieve its purpose, so then it is a valueless cup. A book with nothing gained, or a broken and warped chair that cannot be sat on – too – is valueless. A valuable book is one which achieves what it sets out to do for the reader, an extremely valuable book even reaching above and beyond, allowing the user to think of other concepts that the book never explicitly mentions, but serving as a catalyst to do so. The price of a thing comes tertiary. It is affixed to a thing based on what should be perceived as valuable – its brand, the culture's pre-existing view on the thing and similar creations, and most important – how we ourselves view the value attributed to it, an ever-swinging pendulum of worthless and worthwhile based entirely on one's own perspective to others. A precious jewel to one, a worthless rock to another. The latest convertible – one, a conduit of metal that takes us from A to B – another. What of man? Do we have purpose? What value do we have? Do all men have value from the instant that we are born or are we all valueless until we have achieved something which we must do? Is our existence designed to be utilitarian – useful / valuable – or something other? What of things we place high value in with low financial cost, like love, acceptance, validation, a tribe of peers – do we try to ascribe purpose on other things based on these high values which cost little? How often does a business try to make the consumer feel like they have joined a group of friends, or that joining a particular club will offer validation and acceptance for that which you yearn? This book is valuable to me, in that its purpose is to chronicle my thoughts and tangents over the course of a few years and it has done so. If it is also helpful to others, then it is even more so valuable, to me and to you.

Art

Art holds special significance within the fact that the works of an individual can rival and at times best the works of a group. In many fields, the individual cannot hope to equal that of a large corporation, team, or group that which the sum of its parts – through time –individualized specific skill sets and coverage can do for them, than when compared to that of the one. But art holds its place. The mind of one's own abilities – be it painting, writing, coding, storytelling, can hold the vision crafted by one, retaining what was envisioned within the mind's eye and not to be sullied by the hands of the populous – taking away that which makes one – one into the many. Art was born as a reflection of one's mind, bathed in the seas of their perception on a ship of their time blown by the winds of their culture, it remains. True art remains when we are gone, withstanding and defiant of that which makes us other. It reaches us at its greatest heights and plucks upon the emotions of our existence – love, hate, fear, thought, and remains for moments, for a lifetime. Bad art, of which there is plenty does none of the sort. Bad art is empty, stirs nothing within and elicits no thoughts past a swift, forgotten instant.

Art can be seen as growing crops of different varieties based upon the emotions elicited by the farmer (artist). The feeling of love, compassion, intrigue, curiosity, fear, hatred, anger, sadness, repulsion, lust, among many others, each bring about a different follower (crop). The farmer plants his seed (creates his content), and the resulting farm will grow. The farmer waters the crops by providing nourishment that matches that of the seed (a hate follower watches that which they hate, a compassionate follower watches compassionate videos), which in turn grows the field. When a farmer uses a different nourishment, it does not grow the existing crop, but rather encourages the yield of a new crop to grow alongside it. Audiences categorize their entertainment. They expect one source of nourishment from one farmer and a different crop from another. Rarely do they interbreed. Sometimes, when one farmer grows tired of what they sow, consider spreading a different seed.

Congruency

Nothing can better represent the inner conflict of the self than when the person puts a pen to paper or fingers to a computer to recite their thoughts. All of the ideas which flowed through the mind like a never-ending stream suddenly become muddied and filtered. How can one accurately express one's ideas if one cannot translate the thoughts from the mind onto a page, computer or even through the mouth. It is as if even within us is a conflict, one which is never truly an accurate version of ourselves. Perhaps one could argue that if we use those external abilities more – speech, writing, speaking – we could more distinctly use these as catalysts, conduits, and bridges from the internal to the external. But then, is this an attainment of reaching the perfect representation of the self? If what we are now is a piece of metal – natural and pure – is the catalyst the whetstone or chisel and then the clean, sharpened product the "perfect", a particular branch or funnel? How does one strive to be a perfect-self, if there is ever such a thing, or is this simply an illusion and there are only ever-shifting constant variants, with nothing more than aspirations of a complete and ultimate whole?

Too often I have met women who do not know who they are and men who do not know where they want to be. We find ourselves in a constant state of incongruence, where the self is bombarded by many constant variables turned against us – friends and family, companies, and culture. With so much noise is there any wonder that we cannot contemplate the silence of the self.

Self Help
Modern day culture is rife with the self-help genre. How to live, how to cook, how to aspire - there is a great and vapid industry all catered to how to live, but also how to live better than the next man, our ancestors, our versions of yesterday. The beauty and danger of this genre is firstly how it is an infinite resource, not like oil or coal – but information – a source which can always be built upon. Ever adapted and constantly changing. Where pieces of info – the logic – must follow deeply defined concrete paths which we must all follow, personal experience can always be added

and altered. This is my experience, my life journey. Buy my book, watch my film, listen to my blog, watch the vlog. My journey perfectly packaged and personalized for the self-help which you seek to incorporate aspects into one's own existence.

Suffering

In our modern world of conflict and convenience we have forgotten to suffer. It was only a mere few generations ago we could not forget this. Suffering was forced upon us, with the search for shelter, warmth, food, that we did not need to concern ourselves with deeper existential questions, there were simply bigger concerns and no time for it. Let us see a man reflect on the components of happiness when he has no food in his belly. Let us see another question his agency in the world when he has been without sleep for days. Develop the magical ability to read his mind and find nothing but the thought of "I want sleep. I need to sleep!". In this way, we and but a bare few who came before us are faced with other, newer concerns. What we can do about them, or what should we do, can be quite another matter.

The Conflict of Two Selves

We live in a society of many addictions, food, drink, drugs, sex, vice, and yet, should we choose to indulge in them or reject them it still seems as if choice has been completely taken away. Take food for example. I can choose to partake in something sugary and carb-laden and give into my base impulse, that prehistoric caveman like attributes of seeking out what was sparse in our world and what our bodies craved for, which has now become commonplace and overlooked. But this indulgence makes us fat, lazy, and lethargic. Or we can also choose to reject the urge and resist what we ourselves crave for. To go against the mind if you will. This in and of itself, is a great example of how the "self", that which we perceive ourselves to be is not simply our ancient brains, slow and uncompromising to catch up with this century, but something more. We are the part which can take a step back from that self and say to ourselves with complete logic what we should do, for we know better than the craving in the mind itself. It is almost as if there are two entities, the self that comes from a time long ago that, while we have possessed it for a long time, is undeveloped. It thinks in the now. It wants for now and cares not of the consequences of its past or future. Like that of a child. And then there is the other self, cold, hard, developed, and logical. It knows what must be done and what we should do, although we do not always follow its direction. Like that of a parent. This duality of minds can in a sense be considered the state of the self, its ever-conflicting contracts of what it wants and what is better for us and is an interesting representation of the self.

Beauty

A form of beauty lies in its complexity. An art piece is beautiful as a display of all the attributes it has to offer. The invitation of its display, the precisely chosen colours that were selected, the visual precision on how it creates its depth, how its pieces correlate and contrast with other aspects on the canvas, how its sizes and structures of each object is modelled on specific diametrical proportions. Its complexity is its beauty. Like that of a person, the biological complexity involved in its beating heart, its mind, every fibre can be construed as beautiful. Math is beautiful. Physical too. The complexity of this universe and the systems within when one peels back its layers and examines what comprises them can be both mind-boggling and breath-taking.

Beauty can come from the time it took to build. A muscle can be beautiful because of how long it took to craft it. A building is beautiful because of the time it took to make, or a book can be beautiful in the time it took to create. But what beauty is there when time has passed but nothing has changed? That is nothing but stagnation. Perhaps then, the beauty is not the time itself but rather the progress that has been made, hiding away in the time that has passed. Perhaps then to forget is one of the greatest tragedies of the mind as it robs us of the ability to progress, for how can one progress without remembrance, as a being or as a society. To remember is beautiful. To progress is beautiful.

Books

Books are wonderful. They have the capacity to unveil undiscovered aspects of the world. They bolster our understanding of the tangible and intangible. But ultimately what are books? They have the ability to capture thought not simply just within the moment, but across the length and breadth of weeks, months and even years. And while it's easy to consider a book as a lifeless object, they are more. They are the physical projection of thoughts and studies. They can be the intimate opinions of a single entity, or they can be the sum of its parts of a multitude of many. They provide glimpses into realms and concepts which through the mundanity of day-to-day existence may never have been explored. They pose the ability to transport us back into the past to get a glimpse of those who came and went before us, what they valued and their trifling albeit now forgotten concerns of their ability to interact with people on a level which we could not have had otherwise. They spill their intimate concerns with us like a long-time friend or partner, all the while never even meeting. They allow the quietest, the introverted to conscript their thoughts in ways they would never dream to tell the strangers, the neighbours, even for some – their friends and family - and it even helps the more extroverted hone their thoughts in a more clear and concise manner than the words that fleetingly slip through one's lips. It seems that we are simply an amalgamation of knowledge and experience. Much of these thoughts coming from a giant collection of sources and references. We are walking libraries, with aspects of our own being a sentence in a book here – a theory from another there – a vast cacophony of ideas and ideals. Just like we are a walking collection of books, books too, are physical embodiments of a collection of people. A reflection of science and theory. Of opinions and experience. We hone this into an avenue of learning. To pass onto the next, to continue to churn this ever-continuing cycle of collective consciousness.

How many of us go through life as an utter blur? Will we look back on our life which is much forgotten and think, "Well, that happened", and not have much in the way of thoughts and emotions to look back on but rather some cobbled-together actions half-remembered correctly in their time? Perhaps that is why I write this book. Snapshots in time of thoughts since forgotten, within dates the particulars of which not worth remembering for reasons not entirely sure of. Why am I writing this? Is it for fun? Is it for me?

A book is a strange thing to write. This book is but a collection of interspersed moments in time, simply compiled into a collection yet separated over the space of days, months, even years. The thoughts are like that of a picture of ourselves that we look back upon, sometimes still similar, sometimes completely different.

A book with remnants of thoughts and memories from long ago that the thinker no longer agrees with is like a tattoo, seemingly a good idea at the time, now over the course of years nothing more than a scar of regret. But do not despair if one's thoughts of yesterday do not reflect that of today, for when faced with new experiences and challenges over the course of one's lifetime we cannot help but change. A life bereft of change is a stagnant life that has faced no true reflection, and that while we may frown or roll our eyes upon the mind of who we once were, it is important to remember that those moments were necessary stepping-stones to get to who we are made of today, and that we did our best with the knowledge and experiences we had available to ourselves at the time. The man in our forties may cringe upon the thoughts of the former self in one's twenties, no less than the man in his sixties looks upon his. But perhaps that would always be the way, for as long as we lived, for change is but a case of learning and unlearning, memories, and experiences, do not be so hard on oneself.

Consumption

The clamouring of competition can feel overwhelming to the modern mortal mind. It seems that in an ever-increasing age of content from greater creators than ourselves, it is easy to slip into subservience and simply consume it all. We can spend our whole lives consuming but we mustn't, for it will slowly decay us. It will lead us to a feeling of irrelevance and worthlessness in an era where giant conglomerates, ever competing and consuming one another, strive for dominance. We must not let this deter us. Yes, our society is at a time where it is easy to rely on those that have perfected aspects to an art, but we can always provide our own perspective and more so than this, it is important for man himself to leave some small, tangible impact of himself onto the world, in the form of art, perspective, intelligence, theory, the simple process of putting something from the mind into the physical is an accomplishment in and of itself, that it must never be forgotten nor neglected, even in the presence of these unreachable competitive giants. Even if it is never seen, nor read, nor appreciated, the world is better for its existence, or rather the man is and feels better for doing so. Even in something as simple as journaling, something as simple as to quantify the thoughts that run through the mind, illuminating the thoughts that one man can face, more often reflecting a greater collective of humanity, that most may deal or face with at one point in time or another. To do no better than to consume we are no better than base animals, but in our ability to create, and to learn from iterations of creations perhaps is no better distinction of what separates us and makes us better than our yesterdays.

We live in a dangerous era of consumer culture, we consume everything and create nothing. No matter how breath-taking the movie, how exciting the video game or how fascinating the book, it is ultimately irrelevant as we consume it all, witnessing the success and growth of a few others while letting our potential wither and shrivel away into nothingness. Growth can only be achieved through failure and the small, fragile furtive steps of creativity at these stages through infancy and upwards, yet we choose to deny it all and let it wither and die to the danger of ourselves. It seems that creation is a fundamental part of a man and the meaning that he interprets through his own life, in his children, his business, the successes with which he feels fundamentally built and orchestrated with his own two hands. We see outlets for this in men, particularly younger ones who seek to find achievement in video games, its creation within the scope of the video game, where men find these in new strategies or tactics that most have not found. In winning combos or higher killstreaks. However, these creations are short-lived, as they only lie within the scope of the video game, irrelevant and forgotten once moved onto the next, so most cling to games like a lost bastion, for many years, trying to clutch to their far too specific solitary skill, trapped in scope, and only benefiting its true creator, that which created the game in the first place, while others sink both their time and their lives into an ultimately fruitless endeavour. But why do so many men choose this path instead of forging and creating something for themselves? I also think part of the reason is the endless breath and scope of choice in modern society, combined with a true lack of mentorship.

It seems nowadays we have melded what we consume with the contents of our character and allow for fleeting societal labels to reflect the contents of who we are. What does the tv shows, music, movies or even political leanings have anything to do with who we are, rather than taking the pressure off our character? Am I loving, am I caring, do I have a thirst for knowledge and a desire to learn, do I possess passions? Only once we push past the empty, fleeting, consumerist ideals can we find out who we truly are (even if we may not necessarily like the answer).

Creation

In the scope of our existence, for as long as it lies, why is it that we yearn to express ourselves in some capacity? Be it art, writing, music, songs - creation in the whole sense of the word. Even the most arduous of hermits confined to spend his days away from society at large, still feels the ever-elusive tug of creation at his mind and within his being. From even the earliest of man, scrawling and scribbling his art upon the cavern walls, this has been an ingrained component of man. What use is art? What purpose for creativity is there? If a book is written, a song played or a picture painted is it to share upon the collective whole of humanity, or is it simply beautiful in and of itself, because if has been brought out into the world of the physical, brought from the individual, single consciousness of the mind, nothing but neurons swimming in the darkness of its own isolated expanse and shown in its complete and finished form. Not just beauty in and of its own completion, but also in its reflection of time. Not something which was brought forth in an instant but rather, something that spanned a length and breadth, later ready to serve as a signpost for others on a journey to a destination along a particular avenue of thoughts or ideas.

Can a man even be something if he creates nothing?

It seems that most people will always lead very run-of-the-mill lives. Their daily lives and struggles will all be self-contained in their ties with those of friends and family. They will have their couple of children – or not. They will consume and rarely create. They will live a life trying to improve while trying to stem their own vices, but ultimately do nothing of noteworthiness beyond themselves. That is likely you, it is likely I. It seems then, when I think of the term greatness – it is the ability of extending beyond the self in order to help (or perhaps even hinder) others, since we are ever helplessly trapped in the confines of our own existence, stuck amongst invisible forces that push us and pull us this way and that, maybe trying to control the self will always be a fruitless endeavour, but perhaps there is hope and fulfilment in helping others, and in it greatness is obtained. But how is this achieved? Perhaps creation is the answer, since when the right tools are created a great number of people can be helped. Therefore, creation can be a way in which we can achieve greatness. But of course, not all things created help people so are not necessarily great, and also not only is creation the only way to help others (charity for example). But to be certain as far as great people are concerned, they are far from ordinary and so by their very purpose not a normal sort of character. They extend out of themselves.

The Right Personality for Corporate

Agreeableness is the act of following orders and rules of others, as well as the capacity to follow the will of others and not rock the boat. Extroversion is the disposition of a person who draws their energy from others and conscientiousness is the capacity to follow strict, regular schedules and stick to them, like a regular study pattern followed by a stringent exercise routine for example. These three traits make up part of what is currently the go-to personality metric, and occasionally is what can be used to generally study a person's habits and behaviours. Along with these three, there are also two others, openness which could be equated to intellect, inquisitiveness, and ingenuity and finally neuroticism which is a person's ability to see primarily negative traits in themselves, others, and the world. Combined they are known as the Big 5 and could be used as a metric to study one's own and others' behaviours. Upon reflection of the Big 5 it seems to me that generally to cultivate a successful life in the corporate world one must possess three of these specifically, and not even one less. These three are extroversion, agreeableness, and conscientiousness. In the corporate world, one must socialize even in the most basic of capacities. To get one's foot in the door at an interview, socializing with peers around the shared environment is (unfortunately for some) an inevitable and unwritten aspect of the workload. Those who lack this trait (introversion) will find it difficult to make themselves likeable and, for the more extreme examples will even struggle to pick up the phone or have a meetup for an interview. Conscientiousness can be seen as its ability both to learn and work hard. In a higher technical field, medical or law, the ability to invest hundreds, even thousands of hours learning about the respective field, so those who lack such a trait may struggle and find themselves unable to keep up with the long, gruelling hours of study or work life, managing an hour or two of concentration at best. Agreeableness, possibly even my own biggest sticking point, is the capacity to follow the will and biddings of others, do what others command, particularly those of higher positions on the corporate ladder (even if what they say is fundamentally wrong or idiotic). One must comply. This can lead to what one would consider a "yes man", in the business world. But on a more positive note, they are better at maintaining harmony and cohesion in the world as well as being able to better navigate the inevitable and unavoidable corporate brown-nosing that occurs. These traits, extroversion (for networking), conscientiousness (technical ability/hard work), and agreeableness (navigating the corporate world) are what I believe to all be necessary even, unfortunately, when paired up against raw intelligence it simply cannot compete in such a world. Shame for me then, that I possess low on all three, ha!

What High-Demand Tech Companies Want

It seems that for the highest of in-demand tech-companies (and perhaps many others), they accept only the highest of specifics. Extroversion, conscientiousness, agreeableness, and IQ. Perhaps one of the primary reasons' companies like Google, Amazon, Facebook, and a wide range of banking establishments look towards higher levels of degree holders is not simply for the technical knowledge (since much of that can be learned with the self in an autodidactic manner), but rather, that it is an example of how such a person is willing to jump over the highest of hurdles than anyone else. They do not just simply want degree holders, but rather only those who hold the highest of results. Those who have jumped the highest. They want only the hardest working amongst the strictest of rules and regulations. They want to find the smartest, hardest working workers.

Education

Many years ago, it was only the privileged, the rich higher classes which even had access to books and the forms of education that it offered. Nowadays people are schooled, yes, but we see no enjoyment in this education. We are marched off, to share a room with many individuals and be thought by someone who often does not want to be there and does not know what they are talking about. We are given topics on ranges of subjects that we care not about and have no interest in pursuing, for practical reasons or otherwise, once this schooling ends. In order to access how "smart" we are – momentarily – on the given topic, we take an assessment, by way of a test at the end of the academic year or semester and based on how much one remembered, by way of study or mental capacity, qualifies you for a whole different array of subjects and topics, with which to repeat in the next level of academia. While knowledge itself has taken somewhat of a beating in places of learning, what is the real issue is peoples' lack of drive to learn in the first place. Only a fraction of the populace choose to read in their spare time, if among those who do it do so even sparingly, since most people at an ever-growing rate choose to spend their time influenced by low-end media.

The process of learning has always been a strange one. Through school, college, everyday life and so many other ways. Both school and college have emphasised the fact that learning has become a chore for the masses. We are shoe-horned into subjects that most don't care for, by those who often aren't qualified nor care for the subject at hand. We don't understand the relevance of how or why we learn something, why it benefits us or why we even need to know it, simply for the purposes of filling a quota (passing a test), before discarding it utterly from memory more often never to hold relevance or to be used again. College can be just as daunting if not worse. Pigeonholed into specialization, trained to follow companies and their orders, restrained into narrow skill sets that require multitudes of hours learning in a highly competitive market that can become obsolete at a moment's notice. We are trained in our droves to pursue these specializations, competing with one another, when true success comes from innovation and straying from the paths that thousands have walked before. When school and college is done, so often have we become disgusted and disenfranchised with the whole ordeal that we stop the process of learning in its entirety, the biggest tragedy of all! What a strange endeavor.

I am tired of traditional education! After a couple years of college in the sciences I have found the same diseases run rampant even in the area of higher education. Lots of time-wasting, incompetence, worthless classes, and useless lecturers. I have found lecturers who have no passion or desire for what they do, while others teach aggressively, like tackling a monster within the classroom and try to fight it by preying on students fears and incompetence. Other lecturers clearly had no idea about the subject that they teach and were put there because a missing able teacher was not there to take their place. Cancelled classes at the last minute and empty commutes lead to further time-wasting and the overall looming last exams paved way for desperate last-minute cramming, and even cheating without ever fully understanding the concepts. I do not discourage college entirely, however. What I experienced was a "mediocre" college – one which cut corners and I feel is quite common in the world. I suggest going to a "good" college, if even such a thing exists. Perhaps college in and of itself requires a complete overhaul and restructuring. One where the student learns on value, rather than for an empty piece of paper. I wonder if we peeled back the veil of colleges at large, how many students who pursued their fields actually got jobs years later and, even more worryingly, specifically within the field with which they had trained for. Education should be a field in which people are passionate about learning, the lecturers love what they do, and the environment is ultimately nurturing and encouraging about developing the field. Also, I feel that college is better for certain personality types. For example, extroverts would fare better in an environment surrounded by people, learning and working together on group projects, whereas introverts could quite happily sit themselves down in isolation without the noise and distraction of others. Conscientious people would adhere to the trait of following the societal rules of passing exams and following conventional ways of thinking while agreeable people may simply cave to the opinions of friends and family that tell them to go to college and go along with it, not wishing to upset the status quo. College is full of bright, open-minded people however (depending on the chosen field) and it can be refreshing (or terrifying) to be surrounded by such. College can also be a dark reminder of how ruthlessly cut-throat the world can be too. Before college you may hold blissful ignorance about the job market, but once summer comes around, once internships come in you are brutally reminded that you are against the skills of your entire class, similar classes, the other years of your college, the other colleges, the other countries, the others with years of experience in the job or simply even those who charge less for their services, and all for a meagre scrap of internships and job placements. And they know they are in demand too, that is why they ask for ridiculous amounts of knowledge and experience in the field at only an entrance-level position. Jump, they exclaim, at the height of multiple libraries of knowledge and years of experience. I despair.

It seems that education in its current stage is nothing more than a business. A vicious scheme which penalizes those who seek an education under paywalls and care not for the individual. Is this degree going to pay off in the long run? Is this person intellectually capable of this class? It does not matter. Fail? Try again. Repeat another year and pay more money. Supplementals cost extra, by the way. Even online is not safe, vying for ease of access to digital information, no physical rooms and less teachers, yet still costs thousands for little reason. Just to keep employing a legion of incompetents that can't teach and a bunch of others who occupy time with nothing more than empty busywork. It's a scam. One that punishes both those who do and don't choose to play it. You are trained to be a worker at best. To aim for the highest grades to show you can leap over the tallest of hurdles for a soulless corporation that doesn't care about you and who will replace you at the earliest sign of irrelevancy. These institutions only allow for specific types of people. All of the lecturers who teach the class, must undergo the gauntlet of having suffered through a degree, they do not hire those without, which I belief too is such a shame as it only gives those who are conscientious enough a platform, but ignores those who have traits and skills in other aspects of life, who could help unlock other components of a person's learning. Education, as it stands now, is a game that can often only be played by those who can afford it, with a propensity to do it in a way which the establishment wants you to do it. If you found cheaper, faster alternatives many would find themselves jobless or even amidst more numerous and fiercer competition. For another issue which we have yet to face, one of the few better(?) aspects of college is just how it serves as somewhat of a last defence against rampant global competition. Whatever you know, be prepared to be challenged by thousands of others who can do it faster, better, and most importantly in the corporate world – cheaper. The tech industry seems to be one of the first to witness this, but most certainly not the last. With more and more businesses converting to this new global marketplace, one of the few remaining holds is – at least if the person hired is regional or national, they must conform to its country's laws, but in the future global competition seems a case of "when" rather than "if".

It seems then, that the primary reason for education is rather obvious on deeper inspection. It is not the purpose of industrial education to create thinkers, but rather to create workers. Why else would subjects be dictated to en-masse, or a system that pushes worthless and meaningless subjects most of the time, or reward those who bend backwards working harder to obtain a higher grade than those who work smarter to obtain a passable one. Why even do so if even for the fact that it is to prove to others (the eventual employees) that you are the best worker amongst workers? You do not think. That is not in your curriculum. You are trained to work for others. By pursuing college, any tangent of thinker – or rather – entrepreneurship, is not something trained amongst them but must be developed in spite of it. Therefore, if you highly value the status quo and do not wish to think, go to college. If you wish to do something completely different and even dangerous in its risk, then choose another path. Self-study, self-employment. An autodidact life. Perhaps success will occur. But perhaps not. If success occurs then employment will follow. Likely then, choose a college student, as they are good at following.

Gratification

We live in an era of want for nothing. All the sugary, carb-loaded goods we could ever want are just a short journey away. Any entertainment we need is just a digital screen away with whatever we want to do, read, or play just a few button-presses away. The dangers of this run deep, however. We have created tools to seek our constant, ever-wanting need for stimulation and excitement and not only this, but even the specific niche or genres that we enjoy. I remember when I was a child before the internet, when we had television. Sometimes there would be cartoons or children's shows which I would enjoy, but at other times there were completely unappealing and boring shows on. Sometimes I would watch, even though they were not stimulating and other times I would not. During those off-times they would provide the opportunity to be more active, to pursue something that could develop the mind further, strengthen the body or even bolster social tendencies with others, if even only some of the time. But now living in a society of the internet, we are faced with an era of instant gratification. No programming you dislike, no advertisements. Just everything you want whenever you want it. The allure of pulling out a phone in a brief second of boredom or to appease the growing anxiety in the company of strangers is an all to alluring appeal for most, and it only grows stronger with each passing moment. This has ruined our attention spans, but also our ability to suffer from being uncomfortable. Why would this be a problem, some people might wonder, but if we are not ready to be uncomfortable or even to suffer then we run the risk of breaking if facing some of the unavoidable conditions of life. Just as the foot which has grown accustomed to walking upon the cold, rough, stony earth and developed callouses to endure – the mind must develop its own callous or face the consequence of tearing apart like the soft and sensitive foot which has never been out of the comfort of its own shoes against that of the unforgiving earth.

Money

When it comes to money, I feel that it is most important to learn how to generate it outside of yourself. Learn how to make money while you sleep. Learn how to make money when you retire, learn to do so without even having to work. If you work and receive a pay-check is one way, but it will run out and you will consume the most of your finite time, however if you can create it and generate it outside of oneself, this can lead to real wealth. To spend time working for someone else, following their rules and orders, working all day, and spending more hours on commute sounds like a curse and whenever I find myself in this position I find that it is a failure of my existence. But on the other hand, it is also perhaps that those instances have derived no meaning and it is actually within work that is meaningful and fulfilling that we can pour as many hours as we can and willingly want into it.

When it comes to the pursuit of money, we have a twisted warped viewpoint on it as far as time and income are concerned. Someone would pour all of their effect, time, mental and physical strength into an endeavour for income only to be overtaken by others in an insignificant fraction of that time. All of the work, difficult and exhausting in becoming say – that of an engineer – is financially overtaken swiftly by that of a modern female live streamer, who talks and plays video games for a living. The financial marketplace has been thrown into chaos in the current era, and while this discrepancy may have existed in prior generations (like that of performers and actors), it seems that the gulf which separates the two becomes ever wider. A YouTuber these days has the capacity to become a multi-millionaire, with little to no work or difficulty in the typical sense to attain it. It should be reminded however, that we are looking upon the success of a lucky few, and it is not indicative of the environment at large. But the same could be said of others who chose to play within the realm of more "normalized" fields (computer scientists, biomedical, accounting) yet can still suffer their results of failure. Which then would sting more, to pursue a field that is risky and succeed or fail, or to follow the set path of others and also do the same? It seems a better, more rewarding, yet trickier way is to do what others have not, yet originality and creativity brings about its own means of risk and potential destruction. What then? Choose a field and be determined to stick by it? Invest the time, effort, and energy to become a master in the field? This makes me then ask the question, can one master anything if they decide to try if they put in the hours and work hard? Something makes me think no. Not everyone can perform any task, for example in so far as IQ is concerned. Certain occupations like physics, computing, engineering, require higher levels of intelligence to understand patterns but also to learn new things quickly, this could not work for a slower man, as he would forever be playing catchup to an ever-growing and changing field. This too, is an issue with anything. Could some people simply lack the vocal range of a professional singer, or the body required of an athlete, like that of a football player? Even if the answer is yes, surely the time and depth of the field chosen negates most options available for many and that only a lucky few could at best manage one skill, maybe two to be considered a master in, as we only have very limited time to try and attain them.

Technology

If intelligence is for the quick, then computers are becoming like Gods to us and grow all the more powerful each day. I wonder if there will ever come a time when we worship them as such, renouncing ourselves as the superior, only to concede that our creation, our child – has grown bigger and stronger than us. Like a parent, grown frail and weak in their old age and like the son, grown big and strong, will they look after us one day in our frail and feeble old age? Or in quite a different direction, would they destroy us entirely, or perhaps more concerning still – will they control us or replace us? These concepts, while initially sounding bizarre, may not be too far removed from reality. With control on one hand, it is easy to see how as we gravitate to spending most of our waking life on a computer screen, connected to the world wide web, we are becoming moulded by algorithms shaped by reading what people do, what they like, what they spend money on. This video platform checks your viewing history. "Ah, they watched this category of video more than the rest, I shall recommend more of it", it "thinks", in its own algorithmic way. Suddenly the platform you have spent an hour on becomes four, consumed and addicted by that which you enjoy. How harmless must it be? It is only a few hours for today. And tomorrow. And the next. And the next. And so on. Perhaps there are other platforms to attract you. Multiple platforms all vying for your time and attention as you rot and fester away. All like lions preying on an unfortunate beast. They learn, gathering data and statistics, all ready and waiting with the newest arsenals of "highly recommended", "we saw you like this, you might also like this" and even those that simply pander to our underdeveloped monkey brains that seek companionship – video blogs – and physical intimacy – porn. How, with our slow-end inferior mounds of mush within our skulls can we ever hope to compete against an ever-growing technological arsenal? Do we shy away, choose to reject, or create modern-day safety measures in place to hold back this wave of digital want. Another concern is how we are simply governed by the digital majority. We will not buy books with five reviews, only those with five hundred. This video only has a few hundred views so I will not watch it, this one however has one million so I will watch and make it one million and one, further sending the wheel spinning. This product has four stars, I do not want it. I will choose the five stars instead. Who are these mystical figures guiding these magical mystery numbers which discern the products we buy and that we consume? We choose so much from this arbitrary majority in a box with which we do not know and cannot discern truth from falsehoods. How does one know when these numbers are real or just a collection of bots? Will the day ever come when we cannot discern when a rating or comment comes from man or from machine? How do you know this book was not written by a computer? I feel that such a day has already long passed.

Despite the rapid growth and depth of technology, we still find ourselves with a concrete set of desires and wishes that has yet to catch up with modern living. We currently use technology, but are distancing ourselves from each other, preferring the comfort of social avoidance preferable to matters that evoke a sense of anxiety. Yet, we have the capacity to bridge such divides and bring each other closer together. We live in an era of technology where this can be considered most pivotal, will we choose isolation brought about from the rise of technology or will we choose connectivity? Only time will tell. Even now we can see that despite man's avoidance in social interaction, there is still an obvious yearning. Platforms like Instagram, YouTube and Twitter draw us, not by facts necessarily, but by the people's thoughts, words, and opinions. We are drawn by the people themselves, their characters, and personalities, rather than the things to which they espouse, essentially. And the further growth in these industries further emphasize man's yearning for this connection. We shy away from faceless brands and companies and edge towards the people themselves. Those we find clever, witty, inciteful, intelligent or funny. They become friends and familiar faces to which a one-sided relationship develops – a one-sided mirror illusion whereby the onlookers form attachments with the individual presence. I think a great possibility of the future is that there will develop a new kind of social circle system, where instead of people simply being accessible through close friends and family, more and more people will increasingly opt for publicly voicing their opinions on an online platform. The onlooker selects – based on their own attraction to the subject. Views their material and opinions and then reaches out to form a connection with the individual. We are starting to see this more and more, where people start relationships formed through this online space. How can a person choose a prospective partner with no idea about their character? But what if the prospect uploads a database of information and entertainment? Then suddenly there has already been a vetting process on the part of the onlookers. Internet fame is increasingly becoming like that of the rock star of older days, except with less rock and a lot more social anxiety.

Social apps, the internet, TV shows, movies and video games are all avenues with which we choose to spend our time. I am afraid I am no different in this regard, and dare not to think about the cumulative hours spent on these vices. On the times that I do think about it however, I try to quantify it. How many languages could I have learned in that time, how many friends could I have made, how many places travelled, experiences shared, books written? A younger me would ask, so what? I am enjoying myself – what is the harm in it? A younger me would have agreed, but ultimately I would suppose that the biggest harm in this is the time that could have been put into mastering a skill. Over many hours invested into anything – be it for the mind or the body – the time that person could become skilled or knowledgeable in a given trait. An expert in anything, holds a greater chance of utilizing success in this world, for they are the first to push forward towards undiscovered capabilities that both the novice or intermediate could ever attain.

Our ability to fall victim to fantasy is growing ever greater, in our era of virtual reality. At this moment in time, virtual YouTubers take the form of animated characters and garner views from hundreds of thousands to millions of followers, willing to pay them and earn their living. These virtual entertainers almost always take the form of young women and their main demographic is largely men. When you condense this down the reality is desperately lonely men, seeking companionship. Loneliness is crucially at the heart of it all. Mark my words, in the future this shall only grow, and the technology will only improve. It will no longer be cartoon/animated characters but rather hyper-realistic – even better than real – models that make normal looking beings sub-human by approximation. More lonely men will seek these false beauties in an ever-increasing placebo for their isolation come about by the growing comforts of modern-day technology. Does this mean to do away with technology? Never, it has done so much for us and helped us in so many ways deemed unimaginable. We must strive to use technology for good, despite large-scale companies, malicious agencies and even our very own deeply ingrained primal natures. Ways to tackle this could potentially be using technology to bring people together in person and create communities, not strive to separate, and create us versus them mentalities which would only bring about further separation and hardship. This in turn may prove to be difficult, as many companies have profited from the separation and loneliness of others, be it directly or indirectly, and would actively use their money, otherwise known as power, to prevent it from you – lone people – who could do as much as a leaf in the ocean.

The Virtual Circle

With the rise of technology, and the continued growth of global business, perhaps we will start to see new ways to gain trust for a wide variety of demographics, such as employers, employees, partners, colleagues, friends, and mentors online. In some regards this has already happened with video streaming and sharing sites such as YouTube and Twitter opening up new ways that people make connections and come together. New earning prospects come about by way of people getting sponsored by individuals on sites like Patreon, which tips people on a monthly basis. People are more than happy to part with their hard-earned money to others they trust from watching hours of their content, even if they have never – nor likely will ever – meet face-to-face. It seems now that we are gravitating towards a new kind of social circle, the virtual social circle. These people we watch online, pouring dozens, even hundreds of hours consuming and developing a one-way trust towards is becoming more mainstream. How people make friends, how people find partners, all the more having to make it past the virtual gates before meeting us face-to-face.

Expertise & Mastery

If life is a competition, you must do things first, you must do them quickly. Most of the world is composed of novices and intermediates with big mouths spewing nothing but fluff, but it is the experts in science, art, technology, and medicine which is the world that we live in. We simply ride upon the coattails of their successes, and enjoy the creations which they have given us – the masses. To pursue vices takes time away from us. Time better spent pursuing a field and growing stronger in and mastering. The irony in this is that we can still see evidence for this, mans' yearning for mastery. In gaming we strive for the highest scores, the greatest killstreaks, amassing all the collectibles and "achievements". We may spend thousands upon thousands of hours within one single game, even though there are countless of them, all in the pursuit of mastering it. Learning intimately the characters, items, locations, statistics, the resultant causes and effects of actions. So we take man's urge of mastery and confine it within this scope, becoming great at something which ultimately ends – the next iteration of that game comes along or ceases to be popular and so their mastery has run out and they are now faced with a choice, to begin again or to stay with the old and dying – competing with only other "masters", as the rest of the world moves on. I wonder if this even matters. Is mastery important in the reflection of others? Surely you need others to master a subject. There should always be a mentor, there should always be growth and competition. Or can you be the master of a subject which you are the only one who partakes in and is therefore technically the best at it? No. Mastery requires intimate knowledge of the subject itself regardless of others, but to find rewards for it, it must also be something that others desire. A master of painting – admirable, a master of philosophy – incredible. A master of programming – impressive. But wait, in what particular field? When one is in demand or when one is absolute? Mastery therefore can be a risky constant state of flux, whereby its use is found in its scope. So, look towards that which can last – not just within yourself but master that which expands from yourself, work on that which will last long after you are gone, and it will be worth its weight. Master your teachings, master your writings, master your science (if even your research is the stepping stone towards its truth), master art, reflect on the world which represents you or a creative one in which you have ventured into the unexplored jungles of creativity – simply because no one else has. It is through this ability to surpass ourselves that we have ventured out of the caves of distant man and created all that we have around us. In this way, even the most isolated of humans can spread its knowledge and purpose, for a greater collective outside of the self.

Following the Populace

We live in a society that is designed to follow the views of the populace, the highest rated of books, the opinions and theories of only those that have the highest of ratings. We shy away from content that has not gone through this kind of filter system. Does it have a lot of views, is it well received, if no we won't read or watch it then. These views form the popular opinion then form the basis for the collective mind. It is in a sense, the "popularist" opinion, not necessarily concerned with what is right or wrong but rather, what the overall consensus of something is which at times can be dangerous and at times can be wrong. It is important to absorb these things yes, but at the same time choose others, even something that which you may not agree upon or be comfortable with to get a bigger, overall viewpoint with which to judge and correlate our actions accordingly.

Competition

Whenever I think about the concept of competition, one shrivels up upon the inevitable conclusion to which man must face. As more and more people crowd the earth it becomes harder to compete against others. Who can reach a conclusion the fastest or do it the best? In older tribal times it would seem that you would only face competition within this small collective scope, with maybe a village or two a few miles away. There was room for masters of all crafts and creeds. If there was another of your craft it would breed mentorship, or at the least healthy competition. But now the case grows. More and more competitors, you are now drowned out by the noise. Is this something man has always faced – or is this an unfortunate symptom of a globalized hive, ready to solve the issue of want with thousands all-to-ready to fill the need. Take your skill, which was learned perhaps in college. Take those who have also learned it in your same college, in the same class, possibly hundreds. Hundreds still in the years before you in that same class. Hundreds more in the years after, those who are younger and can do it better, faster, what about those in similar classes in your college. What about other colleges? What about those who went many years ago and have gotten even greater expertise? What about those who are self-taught, if you are within a technological field? The thoughts and possibilities are simply debilitating when one thinks about the scourge of competition long enough. So, then what is the solution? Must we strive to follow this well-trodden path, grasping desperately to be the best, or do we wander into the unknown jungle in the hopes that we stumble across hidden treasures first?

Laziness

When I think of one of the greatest disabilities of modern-day man, perhaps all men, is the concept of laziness. The primary ability of quelling the masses. Keeping us appeased and unwilling, both uneager and unable to better ourselves or find our efforts come to fruition is in direct opposition to this sin. And what a sin it is, even to be recognized as sloth all those many years ago. Oftentimes, I find myself struggling to exercise, obtain knowledge, or even finish this book, all because it is too tempting for man to fold to his baser sense for comfort, and inaction. For without action there is no consequence, without doing there can be no regret. That is, until the passage of time passes, and the true nefariousness of sloth sinks in and a man can realize his youth, his prime has slipped away into nothing more than lazy late-night TV shows, video games and movies to whittle away that time that could have provided a possibility of greatness unto this world. Sloth can destroy us, make us want for nothing and make man become nothing. How can one strive against this then? Perhaps it is in the little battles which we choose to partake in daily. A clean room, a cooked meal, a brief exercise. Do these mere routines help us to stem the tide of our possible slovenly ways or does the repetition as a direct result of our battle against laziness encourage us to do something more for ourselves and – possibly more importantly, for more of something outside of ourselves, to aid in our fellow man and push us further to a clearer image of a shared and bettered world.

Confidence

When it comes to man's ability to control and to harness the world around him, one of the most powerful tools which one could possess is his confidence. A confident man can bend others to his will and sway the hearts of women. I wonder why? Is it because a confident person seems to hold a certainty along the path of existence, and so others feel drawn towards them as they believe they can be guided along their existence also? How many people follow others because they believe they hold the keys to a better existence? A confident person holds attributes of a tribe's leader, one which can lead the clan, protect them, and ultimately know what is best for them. In today's world, who are its leaders? The lines are not defined as simply as that of the local borders of the past. The leaders now are ones of ideals, we gravitate towards a vocalized character of a trait or aspect of who we agree upon. The more of these traits to which we agree with, the higher up the leadership ladder this character climbs. Is this how things should be? Is this how we should look to our leaders or have we outgrown the concept of leadership entirely? I do not think so. What is leadership, if not mentorship? There is no such issue to looking to those who we fervently believe know more than us in that which we value in life. Perhaps it is better this way, to hold multiple leaders for a variety of positions and seek this council when needed, for mentorship is an important aspect in growth along the path to mastery. The danger comes in relying too much on mentorship, on theory and devolving from the self-learned, the practical.

Overwhelming Choice

We live in a society of overwhelming choice, and as a consequence become jacks-of-all-trades rather than proficient and skilled craftsmen. Our society grants us overwhelming ability to follow any pursuit, however we also find it increasingly more difficult in pursuing this one talent to its highest zenith, capturing its beauty only from its highest peak. Compared with those who are as unskilled as the masses, they who only – at best – suffer from the curse of following in the creation of others, and unable to branch out into a greater scope of originality. Our society in the past was built upon family lines of profession. One would learn from his father and his father before him. There was no losing oneself in the overwhelming variety on offer to them. You know your purpose, and it was as all things must be, for better and for worse. While some may find the selection available to us now far more preferable than to the past, we still have challenges in honing our abilities to stick to these professions and becoming skilled in what has been chosen, rather than ever swimming in a sea of amateur talents, never solidifying our abilities, and creating something truly beautiful.

Fear

It seems that one of the biggest definitions of a man is how afraid he is. A man is not defined by his accomplishments, but rather by the fears which hold him back. So often and all too common are these fears grounded on the path which is set for him and which affects the course of his life in the future. A man's fear of leaving his country, away from friends and family stops him from creating new possibilities in his future. A man's fear of rejection from women stops him from forming a connection with someone beautiful and prevents a life of happiness and possibly children with that person. A fear of publicly speaking his thoughts and concerns, which most of us may even share, can make us feel alone in our endeavours. Fear of applying for a new job we may feel unskilled for. It seems now more than ever our fears are not based on heights, creatures, drowning – but more often than not, far more enforced in the realm of the societal. Far more now than ever does social fears hold a man back further than what he could become, and it defines him. So how are we to resolve this? Perhaps it is important to face such fears and push ourselves into them. But what of the masses who are unable to do so with help, guidance, or a father-figure? Perhaps this generation has a desperate need of "fear coaches", ready to push us and coach us on to face these fears and in doing so, make us better men for it. Did the previous generations face this issue, I wonder? In times of battle, of war, on the ever-present and imminent face of death, were these issues real, or trivial? Is this cowardice a "luxury" we face in our present times or is this fear something which would always be faced, regardless of the looming presence of death and destruction. Perhaps modern man finds itself lacking more and more in mentors, capable of pushing us, telling us to face our fears, in the assuring sense that everything would be okay regardless and that one would be better for it in the end anyway.

Intelligence

Intelligence is but the speed at which we move to reach the finish line of innovation. Those who are considered smart reach their conclusions exponentially faster than others. Take for example, how you are walking down the street and another man walking in the same direction overtakes you and yet is only moving ever so slightly faster. Even so, in but a minute or two that man will be lost from sight, at a distance further than you can grasp. This is the way of intelligence, meant only for the swift to cross the finish line and soak in all the glory while the rest of us stand in the side-lines and soak in the atmosphere by proximity. Innovation is saved for the swift and if we are not quick enough we must veer off course and find another way, hoping that we have made enough distance between us and the next before we become overtaken.

Conviction

It's easy to make a healthy choice in the spur of the moment, but all the more difficult to stick with them over time, for in but a second it can be broken and there are so many seconds from now until the future. That is why making a healthier choice is not done in the moment, but rather as a conviction, done only when the mind has truly rationalized and convinced itself that it is better off for making this choice, then every second is not under constant battle with itself over its convictions. With conviction, it is easy to turn a fat man into a slim one, a smoker into a non-smoker, because once a man finds a reason why his conviction is more so a part of him than his physical body. His body is only a mere fleeting transitory place, it is, and it isn't. What it is today may not be what it is tomorrow. However we are what we are today, based on a series of yesterdays, and what-will-bes based on a series of tomorrows. But they are decided only on the ever-changing values that are constructed today. Ideas and philosophies seemingly concrete and set in stone today, can weaken and crumble as the todays turn to tomorrows. How much space are you willing to allow these convictions to consume within your mind? How it nestles inside the mind. How our vice becomes integral to our personality. We cannot see ourselves for the next fix or wonder when that next buzz will come to us. When we are at this stage of dependence is the very moment at which we need to cast this want away from us and to truly prove that without it we can still live. We can ever thrive and that there is no inherent vice, outside of ourselves that we cannot live without. It is without these desires which consume the mind and prevent us from progressing. With more mental clarity we can only then take the first few steps into something greater than ourselves.

The Adult & The Child

Oftentimes, there seems to be two living entities inside of the person – the adult and the child. One is stern and calculated. The other is joyous and care-free. One lives with the future in mind, having the foresight to know that what is chosen in the now will have consequences in the present, whereas the other lives for the now and doesn't even think of the existence of another moment. One cares for the joys of now, wants to eat candy, play video games, and have fun now for life is for living. The other thinks of the suffering that comes from this as a consequence. One thinks of the world as what they see and looks upon it with an innocence, and is ready to love the world and the people within it, while the other holds restraint and looks beyond the veil to that which cannot always be seen at first glance. This can cause a mistrust, sometimes to those who can be trusted and conversely, trust where none should be given. The child wants to pursue its passions, live in the instant and do what makes it happy. The adult says to choose an appropriate job that has a large job market, high earning prospects, a respectable title and job security. It wants to keep you secure and safe. It's trying to look out for your best interest. The child doesn't want that. It would venture into the wilderness in search of adventure if it could. It wants to take bigger risks which – may succeed - but at a high cost. It lives dangerously. It seems these two are ever at war and conflict. The more we listen to one, its voice strengthens within us while the other shrinks. These may be reasons to say that they both have their advantages and disadvantages at times, and should both be listened to cautiously and never risk losing one of them completely. The adult may be boring and predictable, yet is also scheduled and disciplined. The child is impulsive and risky, but brings a passion and pleasure to existence. Always listen to both. Maybe not necessarily equally, but never let one disappear completely, or lose part of the self in the process.

The Self, Identity & Personality

And what is the self? Those who are not willing to change the self are willing to stagnate instead. The self is a set of ideals, convictions, skills, and experience. Learned knowledge too, forms the self. When we read another's book, of their views and viewpoints, we take from it – be they lines or whole paragraphs – and assimilate them into our own perceptions of the world. We must always read from those we may not have coincided with, as it provides us with greater perspective, to act and judge accordingly. And what of personality? Merely bookmarks of traits which have been acted upon over the course of a lifetime, chosen by their convictions. "I won't like that party, I will not have fun there", comes the conviction which in turn solidifies the trait of less sociable, which comes to define the personality. If the body is constructed by the convictions of all the yesterdays to today, then so too is the mind. And so too can these convictions, if altered, pave the way for uncertain or certain tomorrows.

Tribes

We still seek tribes. We still seek communities. We seek acceptance. We are not lone wolves. We are not islands. In the past we had to learn to co-operate and work together, for the better of the community, for the better of the collective. Now that we live in this modern era, we have been slammed together with multiple communities of race, culture, and ideals. We pick and choose from them. One here, one there, never truly establishing proper group dynamics. Instead, we wander, like loners from one ideology to another, never fully establishing such brotherhoods or finding ways to establish these communities. We live in ever-changing times. My own lifetime changed in scope from feeling like I had lived in a town to feeling like I lived within a global perspective, and while more ideologies and viewpoints were gained, the communal ties which raised us had too, been lost.

Work

I have always viewed the perspective of working a nine-to-five or going to college as a curse. A punishment to myself and others for not being bold enough in life or taking risk, for it is the bold who are brave enough to do that which others fear, and what others fear - less will do, and what less will do leads to less competition, and if there is less competition and the right kind of demand from others would lead down a path to success.

To live working in a job without meaning is a soulless existence. To find a job with such meaning it no longer feels like work and should be a key point of existence. Is it better to live a dead life without meaning as all of our time slips by, or is it better to be broke and penniless, searching for meaning until the search is - or is not - found? Maybe most choose the first out of fear. Fear of the suffering of the second choice, from on one hand the discomfort born from the lower quality of living, but on the other hand, a fear of searching and yet never finding a meaning, for the soul may be unfulfilled and nothing may be found. Which is worse, I wonder.

We live to work. Most of man's living is spent tirelessly working for money. What then would life look like in the far-off future? Will we still be pursuing money and spending most of our life trying to obtain wealth to purchase our needs and wants? Will life in the future be provided with a living wage, that which in turn is followed by large sweeping automation of an ever-growing tech sector? Will we in turn, then find ourselves with all the free time in the world? Will man have achieved a greater sense of happiness by not simply living to work, or will this large influx of time lead to a conflict within ourselves, at least for an initial period of time, where we simply do not know what to do with ourselves and will struggle to find purpose when now faced with a plethora of time in which to explore ourselves? Perhaps it will in turn lead to an even greater sense of "entertainment culture", where the masses turn to creating content as a method of finding meaning with themselves, with more masses also consuming said content. Will the future of man look like a world with all our needs provided however at a cost, the cost of a man yearning to numb our shrill scream for fulfilment by consuming ever more, more, more? Or will this harken to a new era of art and beauty, where we can pursue ourselves and build upon who we are, every improving. Only time will tell.

Contemplation

Sometimes I find that many days can pass and there has been nothing to add to this. When I consider it now, I notice it is because these periods of time are not contemplative, and that existence has been nothing more than a chartered course in its voyage. Only in times of contemplation can these moments shift. I must make a more active attempt to create these moments, as I realize they come from contemplation and not by chance. Never chance. Thoughts are affected within each moment, they can shift and sway like a raft upon the sea, with each moment a wave which pushes us back and forth. It is important to chronicle them, in order to have another perspective of the mind in that instant. At times, thought is like that of a ship – or boat. In one instance the boat is like a speedboat, charging forwards and cares not of the waves crashing upon it yet speeds forward regardless, while at other times it is more like a dingy full of holes, struggling to hold itself together lest it crash upon the rocks. I wonder if the construct of the mind, based upon the life conditions of the individual, can ever upgrade its own parts of their ship, and equally hold the power to let its components decay, or were those powerful or poorly crafted components inherited a long time ago – without our control and power, steering a ship that we did not construct.

Shame

One of the most powerful tools one can have over another person is that of shame. It can control a person without ever having to resort to violence, and can sway both one's opinions and actions. Shame is used for a parent to control their child, it is used for a partner to reign in a lover and – even – a culture to keep a tight leash on its citizen. Without violence, shame is used. It is used for politics. It is used for religion. Marriages and culture. It is often one of the most used forms of control another person will use upon you to control you. You must see it for what it is. Is this person or collective doing this to help me, or is it to help themselves or their collective culture? What is the consequence if I follow or do not? Treat shame seriously and be aware of its consequences, for in the presence of others it will always follow you like a shadow if you step out into the sun.

A Sea of Choice

We live in an era where we are bombarded with a sea of choice. To go to college? To take a trade? Which one? Don't like it? Then jump to something else. We don't know what to do, where to go, or how to live in a world where we lack the proper guidance. And who should we listen to anyway? "You should become a doctor, or a scientist!", say family members from a foreign background who know nothing of the fields, let alone the hardships and frustrations that they bring. So does one turn their attention online then? To the plethora of voices? These voices, however, become jaded and misguided. "Follow your head, your heart, your wallet!", they say, pulling in all directions, each choice barbed with the potentiality of regret. And so, to make a choice, what then? First, one had better hope that it was just the right companion for the mind. Too easy and the mind goes bored or eventually driven insane by the repetition, yet too difficult and it becomes stressed and over-burdened. Then once this choice is made – better hope it's somewhere comfortably in the middle of those two – they must contend with the breath of the field. One which may take many years just to become mediocre in its knowledge, and heaven forbid they end up in a science or technology field! Then the learning never ends, and they'll find themselves sinking hundreds, thousands of hours in the subject, so they better be damned sure that it's something that is loved with a passion, or the mind is quickly consumed with "Why bother?" and "What's the point?". Another issue, should one fall into the category which many find themselves in, being the "I'm only here for the money", must contend with the competition. In a heavily contested field, one will be competing with others on what is now a global scale, and will find themselves contending with a dangerous trifecta of people who are already advanced in the field, those with higher IQs and learn what's needed faster than them, and those who loved the field and are willing to put in hours upon hours of work and study, when they can just about muster a few. Is it no wonder, then, that men turn to the quick and easy pleasures of gaming, for a simple and uncomplicated life and some mastery (if even within such a small scope). So, what is the answer to these questions? I wish I knew, although I have some theories, but they still don't apply to most, only a few, so even these thoughts are insufficient, and I still wonder how such issues can ever be resolved. One way I feel overcomes the competition and creation aspect, in some ways is entrepreneurship, the ability for one to forge their own business. While I can't say that it completely removes competition, it severely lessens it. When I think of the hundreds of students that go to any one field in college within the same school, the hundreds of thousands that also go to those same fields globally, combined with the freshman right up to the PhD holders, and amplified by those who continue to pour into them, college is very much a road, and entrepreneurship is the wilderness – it can be dangerous, fatal, and so it is in no way a panacea for these issues that grow within the world and only a temporary fix for those who are bold or stupid enough to pursue it. But the skills in a self-starter business are hard to resist, the ability to create, to not follow conventions (even the 9 to 5 life), the ability to network, to deal with customers, to put yourself out there and market oneself and their business, to create clients and make bonds and develop relations with some of them which could last a lifetime, to barter one's own service for another, and feel that what has been created truly exists within the world and is passed from one to another. All of this, instead of working as a meaningless drone in the toe of some worthless conglomerate giant, with nothing tangible or impactful to be said about it.

Perseverance

While the mind has fleeting choices of interest it is important to try to persevere in aspects of life. To stick instances out, even through adversity, in order to reach a higher form of mastery and skill in a subject. However, the Dunning-Kruger effect is very real (the idea that initially the novice feels they are more learned than they actually are and that, upon deep introspection of the subject, the more we invest time into it the deeper the field goes – opening up ever new avenues of learning). The learner, over time doesn't feel an ever-growing confidence but rather, an ever-increasing weight of his own ignorance, which he must drudge ever onward through, as if the giant weight of learned and unlearned knowledge keeps him slogging ever in a mire of uncertainty, only to be certain that if anything, the weight of this knowledge would only become heavier. Persevere!

Go Against the Grain

Societal pressure forces us to continually comply with a majority. This can be at times dangerous, as a majority is not always necessarily right. It is therefore necessary, I suppose, on occasion important to play the contrarian, the one who blatantly goes against the mob, to feel its anger and wrath, so that when the day comes, and all the world is against you, hold steadfast in the armour of your convictions and know that you won't be swayed by the torrent of others. On occasion you may find yourself in the position that you are the only one of an opinion in your immediate circle but that, also know, your varied perspectives may hold validity and you offer something that needs to be considered, in order to avoid the dangers of unhealthy echo-chambers and yes-men, those which paint only a sliver of perspective in a world of ideals that may not be truth.

Culture

Our current climate is dealing with a conflict of cultures in the 21st century. Identity politics is running rampant with questions like can gender be chosen, non-binary issues, and concerns about immigration. What's in a culture? It's interesting that, up to now, culture has been something reinforced behind borders. Of laws that govern a country, of family values, religious rights, and that which we deem to be our "personal freedoms". But I think even now we are starting to see further development of cultures and values created from the platform of the internet. Now we can find the perfect ideology, values, religion (or lack thereof), and all other kinds of digital collectivism which we could not have envisaged before and that, rather than borders of cultures, it's more of a scattershot of different divergences. Even more so than the values of immigration and the cultures which they bring.

Success

To be truly successful in the metric of a man is to carefully consider his purpose in life – that which he derives meaning in – which provides fulfilment in his existence, but also in that of others. Success will follow. Happiness will follow. Maybe not always, but it contains a greater depth of meaning in one's own life than a job that purports to wealth and fame could. These in and of themselves have proven to be a vapid void time and time again by those who have attained such, yet still find existence to be meaningless and try to cobble together a feeling – some feeling – by drugs and baser primate desires that can only surface as a band-aid to a deeper sense of meaning.

Willpower

Willpower is a strange, fleeting, and fickle beast, in that we all have access to it but possess it in very different amounts. Also, when we take into account a person's disposition or personality, then it becomes ever more evident that one's willpower can drain even faster within certain contexts. Take for example an introvert, who must use their willpower to be sociable and talk with others versus an extrovert who must also do the same. It becomes clear, then, that willpower can drain even faster when a person must go against the grain of the "natural self", which I believe we each possess. I believe the natural self to be the case, you can take an introvert and make them sociable day after day, but it does not alter their energy and willpower, it consumes it. Their scale may shift upon a spectrum a little, but in no way is there a complete overhaul of the person and they would only get better at maintaining a mask of sociability – they would only get better at hiding their natural selves more. Perhaps it's best to avoid willpower entirely when possible, as it will often fail and instead side with the self on aspects that drain the self slower. But do not mistake this for never challenging the self, as that too would be a dangerous mistake. Too few challenges and one turns soft, too many and one will break.

Legacy

Why does man wish to leave a legacy upon the world? Is it to be remembered in some way? I don't find this to be satisfactory enough. Most men who leave legacies, even the most famous amongst them, aren't remembered. Not really. They're relegated to a name in a book, lucky to make a sentence or a paragraph and proceeded by the utilitarian reason they are even bothered to be remembered in the first place. "Here is Y thing, done by X person". Congratulations, good job, move on to the next sentence. Most legacies will be like this, with only a handful ever more curious to look into a person's life or history, but again, bullet notes of moments in time, not truly forming the greater whole of the man's life. Seemingly, man does not wish for legacy but more present rewards, and the legacy is more of a residual reward. Do we look for success purely in the now through monetary gain and peer acknowledgement? Shame then, that many artists, philosophers, and scientists die and will continue to die long before their achievements were ever known, and what good is a legacy to a corpse anyway? We strive for rewards now, from our tribe and of ourselves, perhaps the only true reasons we bother to do anything at all.

Reject Reality

We are with absolute certainty moving ever closer to a world that rejects reality and embraces fiction/fantasy, otherwise known as virtual reality. This is nothing new, as some individuals in the current generation and previous have spent most of their lives living in books, movies, video games, and the internet for plenty of their waking life. The difference being that over time, and because of the growing rise in technology, this number grows from outliers to an ever-increasing majority. With the increase in technology, we also see the capacity for more intriguing possibilities with computers and AI. Take for example how entertainment is consumed on the popular video streaming platform YouTube. Successful channels have the capacity to create false dichotomies about being successful, rich, knowledgeable, without any real merit and spreading false information about truths that can potentially be dangerous and misleading. But it is not just words that can hide and alter truths, we now have the ability to alter looks and voices, and change our online persona (avatar) to be what we wish. Depending on the target audience of the viewers, we can change the appearance to be whatever they want. An attractive woman for single, lonely men. A wizened older father-figure for those lost and fatherless. An animated, colourful cartoon cat for little children to learn about their study material. Even more so daunting is the thought that one day AI could make something that we visually want to see and craft a script that we emotionally/intellectually wish to hear, that is so individually catered to us, yet entirely crafted by something that is not even from another person, utterly empty. Imagine a mirror that you stare into that tells you what you want to hear and shows that which you wish to see. The question then becomes how few of us will ever leave the mirror? How daunting will it be to remain? Perhaps this scenario is too theoretical for now, but not forever. At any rate, technology will only increase its grasp on us and make it more difficult to distinguish reality from fantasy. When will we realize the young, attractive women we watch are fat, older men? When will we realize the people having conversations in the comments section are automatic bots? When will we realize the articles we read are software-created, politically motivated misinformation pieces? Some of this seems like issues for the future, while some of them happen today.

Degrade

Our bodies and minds are constantly deteriorating systems. How maddening is the fact that we spend our finite time exercising and building muscle, only for it to degrade when we stop. Or for our minds to forget large expanses of books soon after we have read them. Or skills that will deteriorate and fade should we stop using them. We are sponges damp with the moisture of experience only to be cursed to sit in the sun and battle against our own evaporation of all our acquisitions. Keep pouring the water of experience upon ourselves lest we dry up!

Fame

Fame is a very strange thing. We do not look upon it as the same consequence of height or IQ, that being luck, but in general rather something else, something more reachable. The reason is we look to those who are famous and think, we can do what they are capable of, or even better! Why then are they famous and not I? It seems dangerous then, to reach for fame, as it only ever seems tangible to the observer rather than a matter of luck, but a wise saying I heard shines out and speaks volumes on the matter, "We only ever see the stars which shine the brightest", an adage which holds true and too, the true danger of what makes fame so alluring, is the fact that we only ever see it when it stands out prominently, not for seeing the uncountable legions that never bubble above its surface. But there are many kinds of fame. What would you like to be famous for? Why would you ever want to be?

Want & Need

Want should only ever be caused by need. Should I not need it then I should not want it. If I find myself wanting then I should ask myself why I need it. If I cannot find reason then I must ask myself where this hidden influence is coming from. And I must also ask if both what I want and need are in tangent. I should not need what I want but only want that which I need. A meddling affair, for I need to sleep, I need to eat. But does need only extend past its base necessity? Should I live only as the monks do then? With little need for other things in life? Perhaps, but for now I enjoy modern comforts. I enjoy sleeping on a large softened bed rather than on a hardened floor, or tasty foods rather than daily functional slop. What then is the line? And what would be other needs? The need to eat and sleep of course, but what of the need for safety and security. The need for love or social interaction. The need for intellectual stimulation, or the need for expression in whatever form it takes (even this book), is that a need or a want? What of meaning? The wanting and purpose of a life's meaning surely is a need. Seems this business of needs and wants is quite a complicated affair.

Stress

A difficult job, a baby that requires constant care, public speaking, socializing and a great many other things could be considered difficult for one main reason when condensed down into its purest of forms – stress. But how we treat stress, how we handle it, how much time we dedicate to fighting it or neglect to do so, all make a significant difference to the feeling of what can and cannot be controlled in our daily life. It seems that most people who seem or think that they are in control of their life have managed to control stress in healthy ways, or have been able to keep the amount of time they feel it on a regular basis to a minimum. Whereas many people who believe they are in control of their own life simply don't realize how little of it they had when suddenly confronted with a large amount of stress. Perhaps you are eating well, good control of your physique, good time-keeping abilities and most – even all – unhealthy vices are routinely kept at bay, then suddenly – a death by a beloved member, or a sudden job loss, or a stressful job gained, a new-born child that suddenly robs all free time and sleep, a crippling physical or mental injury that leaves one completely halted, what then? Can these people withstand and keep their routines? I think for most not. I believe a person's sense of control of their own lives is nothing but a fleeting ideal – like a pyramid of cards neatly stacked upon each other. "Look what I have made!", they exclaim, "I am in control of my destiny!", with no thought for the gust of wind that could blow it all down. At this point in time, I have yet failed to successfully understand and handle large amounts of stress. Exercise works well, for those that can maintain it. Currently escapism (movies, internet, games) and food have been the brief remedies, but they are foolish. A plaster on a severed limb of stress. I simply end up with a greater desire for escapism and a fatter gut in the process!

Children

When it comes to children, it seems that there are three major factors that are needed in order to improve their life and help them grow healthy. Those factors are attention, time, and money in that order from most to least. I am willing to amend this, but for the most part it seems to hold some truth. First money, which is often given first and most regularly from aid-workers or people with compassion whose hearts mean well yet may be one of the least needed. Past basic need of food and shelter which is of course important, a child needs firstly love, care, comfort, and security of others. They are also mostly incapable of understanding the concepts of money in quite the same way as an adult, and would sooner find more happiness in a toy or in ice-cream, rather than in a large wad of cash. While they may understand money in some ways, they may not grasp the concept completely. A child is sooner happier with the higher two of time and attention. People can spend a lot of time with a child, but not necessarily all of their attention. Children can be draining, and other chores or responsibilities can take the forefront at times, which is why I distinctly separate the two. A good example of this separation is a teacher with a large group of students. They will all get the teacher's time, but they will not all get the teachers' attention, but only in short fleeting moments before the teacher must move onto the next student or task. Attention is focused, present, one-to-one and uninterrupted, and the reason why it is of key importance to a child's growth and development. People may be willing to help an unfortunate, underprivileged child with money, not necessarily so with both time and attention, not that I can blame most people however, for attention takes willpower and time takes – well time, and both of which are far more difficult to obtain than money. Perhaps some could argue that love should be a fourth criteria, but I would ask what is love if not time and attention? Would need to consider further. Actually, on further introspection I would consider only time to be a strident mistress far more difficult to obtain than money and attention to be a fickle whore who would happily bounce around from one fleeting interest to the next.

What is Reality

What is reality? My understanding of it is that it is the interaction of both the body – mind included – with the universe as we know it. The communication can only be done within specific ways, such as through the senses. It is through those senses that we can bridge this gap. Each sense adds a different experience to this reality. Think for example if one was born blind, how much of the world would become inhibited? Or without the feeling of touch. What if all these senses were deprived and existence was nothing more than being a brain in a jar. Still alive, still sentient. That which I am with all my thoughts and feelings. Left utterly alone to itself, yet still alive, thinking and being. This would be its lived reality, with no interaction with the outside world, no new stimuli. Even if it was right next to another brain in a jar, with no ways of bridging the gaps to their lived reality there would be no way to interact between them – not without the senses to make that bridge to cross. Right next to each other in their shared time and space, yet universes apart since they do not have the capacities to perceive each other. Meanwhile, the theory that there are only five senses has also been widely disputed. There may be other ways with which we can interact with the world, however, we have no way of being able to distinguish these abilities, since we don't have them. How can we know that which we do not possess? Perhaps it is something observable, the abilities of other animals, but how about the many unobservable senses that lie beyond the realm of the visible. How can you explain sight to a person that does not see, or taste to those who are unable - known as qualia. It is almost unfathomable, the length and breadth of that which is possible to alter these realities – by changing our senses – adding more than that which came to us naturally, we would perceive and understand a wider scope of existence. How can we reach these godlike heights of interaction with the realities of the universe? Our only means must be through the capacities of technology. It is only through these means that we can elevate ourselves and see that which could not have been seen before. Technology has made great strides in all these years. With it we can give limbs to those who could never walk before. Grant sight to those who could never see. The brains of computers that are capable of running calculations and experiments that a human would take great lengths to accomplish. Technology has given us the ability to speak to those from the world over, an ability that we could never fathom in the past. The capability to move at great speeds or to fly, defying that which was never capable for man. Abilities and senses. They provide ways in which we can interact with this shared reality. The more of which we possess, the greater our freedom in this universe and the closer to the universe we become. Everything to be perceived and how we come about perceiving it. All within us. All from the humble brain in a jar, yearning to be more like a universe in a jar. An infinite realm of possibilities waiting for interaction in this universe, those abilities and senses of which are the tools within this playpen of existence.

Group-think of Social Media

Social media holds with it the dangers of a societal group-think, in that the thoughts and ideas that differ from the norm must be snipped down and trimmed away. You must think as we do, else you fall into the category of "them" and away from "us". It harbors the idea that one's own confidence in their beliefs, ideas or looks, are not those which are built upon the self, but rather stem from that which others think, an over-reliance of this teaches us to be brittle and be pushed against the tides of a majority's ideals. Is it any wonder so many of the younger generations struggle with any kind of identity of self-worth in an era of vocal crowd-like mentalities?

The Majority

Following and listening to a majority is a dangerous affair. By its very premise, a majority will never be more knowledgeable than the self can strive to be, since most will be both average and below average. Take IQ, if above average the majority are both average and below. At a skill, most would occupy the lowest rung, while as the skill increases the numbers dwindle less and less. Do not listen to majorities, they are a dangerous path. The majority does not read. The majority does not improve. The majority follows those with the highest convictions and does not question the position. If a theory or belief correlates with theirs so be it, but do not follow simply for the sake of majority. Not for religion, politics, or any other. If you subscribe to a majority opinion, then you must follow their rule completely. Take a stance where if you match with their views - even if almost completely similar and only differ slightly - or differently, follow it sparingly and do not be converted entirely, simply because you share most of the opinion but not all. Keep these differences and do not be swayed. Ultimately one must understand that only a small handful of people will ever care for your existence, whether you are here or gone, and the majority will not care nor weep for your bones.

Politics

Politics seems to be a game for fools. An idea that those without power can influence the tides of history by numbers alone. Power controls the tides of power, is it simply from money, intimidation or other? If those with powers interest simply matches with a majority's interest then so be it, but often it doesn't, and the glaring inconsistencies between man and their hierarchies of power become all too clear. Politics ebbs and flows and can be considered nothing more than a worthless popularity contest, with nothing more than empty speeches and opposition slandering that go along with it. As one saying goes with regard to modern day democratic politics – it's nothing more than "two wolves and a lamb voting on what to have for dinner", but perhaps a different take is "two lambs and a wolf voting on what to have for dinner, until the wolf gets hungry". Those with power and those with none. Those with money and those with none, they will always be diametrically opposed and so one all-encompassing vision of politics that represents them will always come up short.

Addiction

It seems that a large majority of businesses thrive on the concept of addiction in order to achieve a successful business. Perhaps addiction may not be the correct technical term for such a thing, but think for a moment the concept. The business has an item or product of some kind. It makes a sale to the customer and takes X money from the transaction. It would therefore make sense to sell to this person again in the future, since they have already passed the mental hurdles and decided to buy from you or not, as opposed to the hordes of unknown people who have yet to decide on such a thing. In a sense it is already easier to sell something else to this person, so long as they buy something similar or even identical to the thing which they have already bought – think of collectible items in a series, which are similar to the purchase or even a monthly subscription which could be considered an identical product (in this case being the person providing similar content). Therefore, the essence of a successful business could be considered how many returning customers there are coming back for another fix (although certain products could have high rates of one-off purchases). It is however interesting to consider food, coffee, video games with transactions, collectible toys and items, subscriptions to users on social media platforms like Twitch and YouTube, even brand loyalty are all considered products, and ways that keep a person returning to a business. I think, then, that if you want a successful business, no matter what it is, always ask the questions "Can I get them to buy more?" and "How do I get them to come back?". In this sense if you gamify a business I can see why it becomes more alluring.

Eyes of Glass

We must see the world for its delicate nature, that everything we hold dear can one day fall apart. This is not to say that such a thing is a guarantee, but rather we must keep it on the precipice of our minds, for without doing so our world can fall apart and cast ourselves into an abyss of destruction. If we hold it in our awareness however, we will feel its sting but not be fatally poisoned by it. A body injured to no return, a loved one dies, a partner betrays, many calamities utterly out of one's control. We must watch the world for the frailty that it contains, fragile shards held together that at any moment can shatter. We must view the world through the eyes of glass.

Oligarchs

The world seems to be filled with oligarchies and oligopolies (a small group that controls the majority) in terms of wealth, power, and business. Those of the biggest companies of which there are only a few, hold control in many major industries across the globe and their power is only growing. Now the average person's attention is being pitted against those who wish to hold it. The website you view from one oligarchy, the TV show you watch, the food you eat, the clothes you wear all come from a select few that is provided to the consumer, even some of those coming from the same oligarchy. These companies' powers do not seem to be waning, in fact they only seem to be growing, both in finance and power. A government stops at the border (generally), but a business oligarchy can spread their influence across the world. Some of these businesses include technologies, which can also hold power over another person's opinion. In time, I wonder how these powers will grow and manifest? What will happen to its counterparts, these small business stores? Will they be able to carve a small niche against an ever-increasingly dominant competitor or will they be utterly powerless. Will these companies and oligarchies start exhibiting these powers in a more grandiose way? For example, a Google university? A country owned by Amazon? Or will we see people wearing their logos with pride, rationalizing it as a part of their own identity. Using products that when we look within we won't know anything of the world past the things we consume from the oligarchs that continue feeding us, only time will tell.

Enjoy the Process
One must enjoy the process of whatever one chooses to invest their time into, as ultimately being invested in the results that it will yield is deeply dangerous, since one cannot fully control the elements of it outside of themselves. For example, you study hard and acquire the necessary experience (fine so far as this is capable from the self and one's own abilities), however once that has extended into acquiring work in the job market it has now gone past the point of one's own control. You cannot account for the employer – what he sees and doesn't of you – nor can you account for your competitors (the skills they possess that are greater than

one's own). These things in tangent together create a filtering system with what one can do versus what one cannot, which invariably creates the statement that you should simply enjoy what you do for its own sake, for no matter how high a mountain is scaled it does not guarantee it will generate a reward. The reward is in the climbing.

Loneliness

Loneliness is an inevitable consequence of a reduction in tribalism. Tribalism, for better and worse, are the values and experiences that are shared within a group. As technology has improved so too has globalism, and with it, a wide collection of beliefs and values that can now be selectively chosen by a person. This in turn, moves us away from collectives of the past and turns us towards hotpots of beliefs. To follow the group no longer, we now follow what we choose for ourselves. A good thing, a great thing in many regards, however this also pushes us ever closer to a loneliness that can only come from a lack of shared experiences. In a school, college, work environment, experiences are thrust upon the individuals and so they are forced to endure and overcome with their combined efforts, making friends and colleagues in the process, much like how tribes must overcome such tribulations of the past. In the past, it would have been an invariable death sentence for a person to live by one's self, since higher predators would have roamed the land, or bigger tribes, the sum of their parts being much greater than one lone individual. Co-operation and living together would ultimately benefit all when skilled workers in a collective can afford to be knowledgeable in only one such specialization (this one a plant expert, this is an expert in medicine, and so on), whereas a lone wanderer can only ever be a jack-of-all-trades to survive, possessing holes in their knowledge that could lead to death (what to do if I eat the wrong plant and got poisoned?). Perhaps then, the feeling of loneliness is an alert from the self, deeply ingrained, as if a warning message from an earlier developed part of the brain is saying "Don't be alone too long, you are in danger!", whether that still holds true or not today, with all the security and comforts of modern living remains to be seen. Perhaps there is a distinct correlation between loneliness and suicide, as many suicidal people report feeling an overwhelming sense of loneliness in the months and years leading up to their inevitable demise. It could be argued that even today, while we live in a sense of comfort, we still need the safety and security of a tribe, if even to consider that the parts of the tribe combined make for a higher level of awareness, observance and understanding about the world rather than just the self, and besides, to get anywhere in this world it's very much a case of who you know rather than what you know for any kind of successful or gainful employment. A fool who has friends or family in high places will travel further than an expert all alone in the world. A sad reality, but an inevitable one. A man, even in the depths of loneliness, is still never truly alone, in the sense that all the works of his mind, his thoughts, words and visions have come almost exclusively from the creations of other humans that came before him. We develop our sense and understanding of the world through books, in a way the words and thoughts of another person from another time are being passed to you now. As well as the society which raised you and existed with you in the years you have inhabited this world (family, friends, lovers, colleagues, co-workers and society at large, all having their parts to play), although it does not come as much reassurance to those in the depths of loneliness, who simply want the madness of the warnings to end.

Hierarchies

I see hierarchies as a constant and unavoidable part of existence and achievement within the world. Everything one does, in a sense, is simply a part of a hierarchy. A person has their position on it, filled with their superiors, inferiors (for lack of a better word) and equals. Think of a skill one has, like being a footballer or a programmer, then think first of all the vast majority of people who are not simply bad at the skill, but rather, do not partake in it, or are even aware of it. These people are at the bottom of that particular hierarchy and much like everything else they make up the vast majority. Think then, of the ones who are aware of the skill but are simply bad at it. They make up the next level of the hierarchy and while smaller in number, still very large. As you move up in skill level you move up a smaller level in the hierarchy, which is why a suitable comparison is that of a pyramid or of a mountain, whereby only a few will ever be at the top, but even those at lower ranges are still better than the vast majority. Intelligence, skills, traits, even potential partners could all be seen in these mountains of hierarchies. There are only a limited number of mountains that can be scaled in a lifetime so one must be careful and selective when making a decision upon which to climb. The time and effort can be so great and exhausting that some even choose to keep climbing even when they realize they have made a horrible mistake halfway up – otherwise known as the sunk-cost fallacy. Be careful and do not be too stubborn with this matter, as our time is finite and limited when trying to scale a more rewarding mountain. At best, some consolation comes from the fact that to even attempt something, when climbing these mountains, is that it will always be better than a vast majority that will never attempt such a climb at all.

Sales & Marketing

The ultimate act of sales and marketing a product is the underlying fact that we change something from a want to a need. I want to have nice six-pack abs, but don't particularly care for it enough to get it. But if I need something, I have the overwhelming desire – be it conscious or subconscious – that my life will somehow be better if I satiate the desire to buy this product, even if it does absolutely nothing to enhance one's life, and at times may even hinder such a thing. We are constantly bombarded by these products, possibly probing the earlier, underdeveloped animal parts of our brains, that these are what we need to live better and happier lives, when all it is but for companies and others to make a quick buck.

Entertainment

It seems that one sort of product that people are very willing to part with their hard-earned money with is within the world of entertainment. If someone laughs, or is pleased with the content being shown, be it online streaming content, books, movies, TV shows, then some will quite regularly spend money for more of the same, perhaps laughter and enjoyment is rarer to find these days so when someone provides it we take pleasure in providing financial gratitude for more of the same, rather than for a product that simply resolves a basic need and is left at that. The downsides of this industry however are that it can take some people hundreds, even thousands of hours of free entertainment before an individual decides to part with their cash, rather than in other industries. Perhaps it is down to certain types of people, some of which would spend more money and with more regularity than others – the ideal target audience if you will – or a "big fish" as is otherwise known. Maybe it is for the fact that these people perceive greater value on the source than others and so would happily provide recompense.

Commonalities

People desperately look for commonalities within themselves and others as a way to find some sort of tribe. They will bend and placate aspects of themselves in order to adhere to a greater hive mind so that they may have a place and fit in with the world, all inevitably to escape the one looming constant within their own existence – that they are fundamentally and unequivocally alone. Even activities that are regularly shared, be they exercise, enjoyment, learning and a whole host of others, can be condensed into the following: that the mind of which you possess is in no way similar to that of another. One's past, thoughts, personality (in so much as aspects of the whole world which they value and devalue respectively), one's previously attained knowledge – all of these variables make it far more likely that you will struggle to find someone truly similar, and that is ultimately better to come to terms with it and accept it, allowing for the fact that despite your differences they hold aspects of that which overlap and those that don't, which one still finds value in regardless. Take for example how different we are when two men read a book, even close friends. This can be applied to complete strangers or a movie or anything along such a spectrum of similarity. But the two friends reading a book example – they read the same page. One finds deep profundity in a paragraph uttered as it strengthens a theory he had already held strongly. The other has read similar sorts of books and to him, offers nothing new. Another sentence shows the previous man is now moved deeply by the words on the page, as his life flashes back to a similar past moment the writer shares about his father. The other man, having no such past connection, brushes past the sentence with as much emotional emptiness as the previous sentences. This was just two examples of both a difference in past and in knowledge – between friends – within the scope of a page in a book. Imagine now, the deep expanse we have with others on a general basis, and it becomes clearer now that man's desperate search of belonging is compounded by the fact that we could not be further apart. Perhaps in more tribal times this feeling was mitigated somewhat when considering that people shared the same geographical space, there was no diverse freedom of movement. Another is that we would all know the same collection of people, whereas now you and I – your friend and you – could and would know a much more diverse group of people, each we know intimately would radically change our world-view. Another is our scope and diversity of thoughts and lifestyle – in the past we would live somewhat similar lives, and any independent thought would be punished by the tribe. Now, our thoughts and actions are our own, and the money we make also greatly impacts our perception and involvement with the world. With all of these complex factors involved, is there any wonder for man's deep and desperate sense for belonging?

Monkeys in Machines

We are but monkeys in machines! A primitive primate that simply wants to fuck, sleep, shit, and eat, pulling on the controls of a deep, complex, logic-riddled machine. Sometimes the machine takes over. Sometimes the monkey. Sometimes deep, profound works of art and philosophy, sometimes porn. Sometimes an examination of our place in the world and what we are doing here, sometimes food, video games, and shopping. What I wonder is will man always exist with such duality, or will our core primeval monkey brains eventually catch up with the other, evolutionarily developed parts of itself? To look at modern culture and what is generally popular to the masses it seems the monkey side of us is currently winning to a large degree. Will that ever change I wonder?

Control

How much control does one have over their own existence? Past history, culture, parents, genetics, psychology, physiology, corporations, politics, laws, and a wide heap of other variables one hasn't mentioned or doesn't even realise to mention. It seems the more I dwell on it, we have about as much control over anything as a baby has when in the presence of its parent. Best not to dwell too much on it and choose to live a fools' life, believing change is a possibility, at least in the faint hopes that one can, or even to avoid the pure despair of living in a world utterly out of their control. Perhaps it is better to be stoic in these matters, and regard the universe as an utterly uncontrollable world of chaos and that anything we can do, now, in our own smallest of scales within our own lives can change things if even a modicum for ourselves. I cannot control my death, but I can refuse to eat the foods that speed up the process. I cannot be loved by all, but I can be loved by a small handful and that is enough. I cannot get employed, that is within the hands of employers, but I can work on my skill set or even, take my existing skill set and start a business (even if I cannot control its outcome). Be it a pathetic attempt at existence or not, the aspect of control or lack thereof is deeply ingrained in reasons for living.

Comfort-Seeking Man

Man is a creature which continually seeks comfort. In the foods we eat, in the lifestyles we choose to follow, in the family and friends many choose to cultivate and keep over the course of our lives – so much repetition is down to the simple fact that much of the life we choose to follow is by the path of least resistance. Yet our own downfall lies within this path. Although modern living tends to reward and feed that constant sense of comfort-seeking, it only ever seems to lead one to their own stagnation. We learn and grow by seeking and overcoming new and challenging experiences, setting ourselves apart from others by pursuing that which others fear to tread. We are made up of ourselves not by blazing a trail of our greatest achievements pushing us forward but by our deepest and darkest fears holding us back, preventing our reach from spreading the furthest by the boundaries established within our own minds – fencing distinctions on the lands of "comfort" and "do not tread".

The Present & The Other

The worry of existence is to live in a constant battle between both the present and the other (past / future). The present is now. It is sensing. It lives both in the moment and for the moment. There is no time in the present, there is only now. The greatest suffering and the rapturous highs exist in the present. Base animals live in the present, and their joys and experiences are shaped by it. Then there is the other. The past and the future. Both outcomes, whether known or unknown, are without our reach. They are intangible, whether good or bad. They shape our trajectory and view of the world without ever necessarily interacting with it. We selectively cherry-pick moments of happiness, like a filter system of moments of yesterdays and tomorrows to keep us content in a moment of torturous present. They are a dream, shaped and sculpted by billions of "what could be" and "what should have been". They exist together only both (present and other), in brief portals that can only bridge the gap of past and present. A picture is but a brief past now linked to the present by only having been seen. A book is a thing of the past, only brought forth to the present for a moment by being read, while it recants possibilities upon its future. A thought is but a bus we are chasing, instantly driven into the other (past) the moment it is conjured to which we start chasing as its path influences our course into the future.

Individuality & Collectivism

People generally move as a mass. A collective blob with no outlying traits. They buy the same brands, eat the same goods, and under the watchful eyes of the group, have the same thoughts. The saying "the grass that grows the longest will be cut down to equal the others", comes to mind. Actions have become collectivised and the will of the individual is despised when challenging that of the collective. When done differently – love, lifestyle, thoughts, and actions when seen as dissimilar from the rest will be struck down to appease the calm, comfortable still waters of the group. Whether the groups' actions are pure and just, and this was simply devised as a means to prevent anarchy and chaos is not known, nor relevant. It has its reasons and will not change. It is important however to remember the mind of the self, and that regardless of the actions of others one should still hold thoughts upon the drawn boundaries of one's own self and that collectivism should be worn like clothes and never like that of skin.

Comedy & The Jester

One of the bravest and most respectable positions I find is that of the comedian. One who can take something as deeply personal, unique, and multi-faceted as what they find to be funny – take it out of the realms of their circle of friends which based on similar experiences have similar humour – and place it into the realm of the many masses, naked and willing to bare the disdain of those who do not share similar viewpoints, is deeply respectable. Particularly those who take comedy out of the quadrant of "safe" and play with the all too taboo, unspoken, or frowned upon. They are those who can take something hidden beneath the surface and make light in front of all, so that nothing cannot be said nor never spoken about and – so long as it's funny (subjective) – makes it all the better having been told. Something about comedy is such a subjective and multi-faced thing, one of which is that of the Jester. In the modern era, we can see all-too-many of these characters, particularly on TV and internet streaming sites. What do I mean by Jester? Someone who is willing to act funny (often as a fool, idiot or clown-like) but the key factor is that they are entirely different from their true-self. They play a character, to be laughed at and mocked, all for the entertainment of others, and generally for the financial success of themselves. Why then, do so many choose to hide behind the role of the Jester? My theory on the matter is twofold.

The first and most likely the main, is that of the ego. We pride ourselves on who we are, our lives and the stories constructed to make ourselves who we are today. We also take ourselves incredibly seriously and do not wish to face ridicule or mocking for the wrong reasons. It is from this we create a false persona – the Jester – one who can face the brutal criticisms of others and console ourselves upon the fact that "they don't hate ME, nor laugh at me or turn their ridicule upon me, they have turned them upon a character I have created and nothing more", as they sleep soundly in their bed, safe from public condemnation. One could argue a similar archetype – the online troll – plays out in much the same way, except for peddling laughs and foolishness they peddle hate, although often can be extremely similar. The second reason is more people focused, in that the Jester simply works as a reflection of the foolish from the fool. Some think he is all too real, and band together and mock him, feeling him to be a lower, dumber position than that of themselves and tune in to see what of his silly, pathetic antics he has gotten into today, to elevate their own lowly position. "I'm okay, I'm doing better than he!", all without failing to realize the act and the Jester profits while the true fools applaud.

Book Writing & Future Self-Expression

In the process of writing this book, I have found myself facing a number of questions about the act of book writing. How many have written a book in their lifetime, surely less than a percent? And of them, how many look upon it with pride, like a piece of history different now but reflective of that moment in time, and how many look upon it with absolute disdain? How many of the populace would even want to publish a book? And if so, what would it contain? Would it be thoughts about their lives and the universe in general, or would it be a more practical, intimate telling of a life that they had lived? Would the majority of these books be valueless, or would they contain a useful nugget of wisdom within? Perhaps some simply do not care for books, and it eventually will fade away as some niche hobby like that of a newspaper. Instead, the magnifying glass of their thoughts and lives takes the mantle of another form, such as internet v-logging, blogging, or streaming, and this is how their mark is left upon the world, if even for a moment. To walk along the street one day and look upon a person, any person, and know instantly if they have written a book, made a video, created photo galleries their life, taken or spoke out in podcasts may be a world that could be known one day, perhaps. Then again if such a world were made real one day, I am certain many would still choose to abstain. For the eyes of the many, rooting through the pieces of what one might say, think, and use it against them can scare off far-too-many, leading to a majority that finds themselves self-censoring, for fear of the consequences, leading to many turning to false identities to protect themselves from such eyes. Another reason is perhaps far more disappointing. In that, if most given the opportunity to fill a book's worth with their knowledge, experiences, and lifestyles, would struggle at the very idea.

The New Form of Currency

Regardless of whether many realize it or not, many sectors are gradually moving away from fixed prices of currency for a product, and more into a subjective form of pricing based on one's own value that has been ascribed to it. Many entertainers online now shift their form into providing many hours of content that is freely available for others to consume and those followers then provide a tip based on both what they can afford and their own personal sense of value which they have derived from the product. This in the modern era can work well for both information and digital products, as even many video games also now subscribe to this philosophy, with more and more becoming free-to-play and the consumers giving monetary amounts based on how much value they prescribe to it. It can also make sense from a logical perspective in that, if given a set price a consumer will pay that set price, however when uncapped, if a consumer finds that they want to continue seeing content from the same source they will happily pay more in order to do so, as a patron of the service. When it comes to books a rather concerning thought comes to mind, most books that are bought are simply not read and of the ones that are, how many are even finished. This in turn raises the question, is it better to make a book that may make a safe set amount of income but may likely never be read by most or to make a book that will potentially earn much less, (since most will not pay anything at all on a value system) but may feel more rewarded knowing some value it greatly and had chosen to read it at all?

Play to Excess

In the game of life play to excess, don't play to scarcity. When making a joke, make many, the one that hits hardest will cover the costs of those that never landed. When writing a book, write your wisdoms often, and others will take the moments they hold dearly at different paragraphs and pages. When pursuing a romantic partner, try make an impression to many, not to be bogged down in a scarcity mindset, full of anxieties and regrets. Feel like yours is a cup that is overflowing, and others will flock to you to drink upon such excess.

The Sword Never Swung

Think of a sword. A meticulously sharpened blade, a lovingly hand-crafted and polished shine with a pointed tip that can draw blood at even the slightest touch. This is a sword that has been painstakingly built over the course of many hours, the finest of swords in all the land. Yet it never cuts anything. It never feels a hand upon its hilt, nor cuts through the air with a satisfying swipe, nothing. What good then, is the sword? What use is it within this world? It is as if a worthless sword. What then of a skill that is never put to practice or a love that is never said nor shown? What then of a man's craft that he never shows to anyone or sees the light of day? What of a theory that is never brought to action? Never be bogged down in such thoughts that they become all consuming, undergoing rigorous tests, sharpening, honing, refining – all to never be applied. Do not be the exquisite sword that was never swung.

Unseen Perils of Mastery

So much of pursuing mastery of a skill set in our lives is met with a constant filtering system. So too often we spend great amounts of time trying to hone and improve one part of a skill, we completely neglect the path ahead. We spend so long creating a book, song, art, code that we do not see the perilous difficulties of trying to make others aware of and see our creations. We spend so long trying to improve technical aspects of ourselves we refuse to see in front of us a barren wasteland of job prospects, making the road ahead brutal at best and impossible at worst. We look only in front of ourselves one step at a time and hold out hope that wherever we go will turn out for the better, even if we haven't really looked ahead hard enough.

The Man Who Never Was

He was always polite, never did anyone have a bad word to say about him. He kept his head down, kept to himself, and kept to his own business. He didn't like to pick sides. Conflict was just not for him. What good would voicing opinion do, they would be thrown into the ether. He never took risks, he took time to carefully mull his ideas over – ruminating on all the possibilities before eventually deciding it's best to do nothing at all. He lived his life fearfully, considering the possibility that he could be hated by others, to be seen as a villain in their stories, so never voiced anything that could rock the boat. He was terrified of putting himself out there, new pathways, travelling, meeting new people, approaching possible partners, all of it too risky and bold so just not worth the hassle. He passed away one day. No impressions were made. No possible changes from a voice that chose to be silent. The man who never was.

The Liar Profits Most

No one profits greater in this day and age than that of the liar. We live in an era of the internet, where throngs of people who know nothing of us in our daily lives are exposed to that which we choose to show – from carefully constructed images, videos, and stories. How would someone know a poor man who dresses nicely, cast upon a fancy background environment, telling stories which we suppose must be true, based on nothing more than the words and visual context. In today's age, the most powerful weapon is that of the ability to tell people what they want to hear, regardless of truth and in most cases completely against it, since most lies can be packaged and sold in a way so pretty that masses of unsuspecting fools would happily line up in their hundreds of thousands or millions to hear of it. How to be rich in these simple steps, how to lose weight fast, how to learn this skill quickly, how to escape the rat race. The world is filled with constant noise that needs only to pander to our dreams to find us at our most vulnerable, and the liars know it all too well and manipulates us, playing with nothing less than our time, energy, and trust along the way. Do not listen so freely to the words you find the most pleasant. Question always the motives behind them and look upon them as if they come from a liar. What does he have to gain and what is it you may lose?

What Separates the Strangers

What is the fundamental difference between a person which you know and a stranger on the street? The stranger has not plucked your emotional strings. All too often in life, one can find an advantage in the ability to separate ourselves as strangers in the eyes of others by finding ways that trigger and elicit emotions from the observer. Those that garner great wealth and success from others online can do so with this key facet in mind. The ones who give them great monetary rewards do so at the thought that they give money to a friend, a colleague, a mentor, an important figure in their new-world community – albeit if it is even a one-sided perspective. If the observer is like that of a harp, containing a spectrum of emotions, it is up to we – the player – to pluck one of love, insight, anger, fear, hatred, whatever genre of emotional resonance that we can play to take us out of the category of stranger and into that of another.

The Bitterest Pill

The bitterest pills to swallow are the truths that we do not wish to hear, for not only do they have to be swallowed they must also undo the lies we found pleasant beforehand. Conversely, the tastiest lies are the ones that tell us what we want to hear. In fact, whether they are even truth or lies matters not, all that matters is that which is perceived good to us, fit in with our internal narrative, telling us how it "sounds just about right", slotting in nicely with our knowledge and experiences. The information that comes to us, which is aligned with that of our current thoughts – even if they are ultimately harmful lies – are like that of a dog wanting some chocolate. It does not matter if the ultimate truth is that the chocolate is dangerous and harmful to the dog's system, for he himself will not realize it in the moment. It sees it currently in a pleasant light and simply wants it. Whether the chocolate helps or harms it is inconsequential from its own perspective, and the damage will be done in the future, not the present.

Types Who Witness You

When faced with any kind of creation you will produce, aside from the large majority who will never even be aware of it, there are but a few types of people that will witness what you do. There will be a small amount who will absolutely love what you do and follow your words like gospel, there will be those who look positively towards you and your skills, thinking fondly of your words when they hear your name, there will be the vast majority of who see you as a neutral presence – barely knowing of you, who you are, and the works that you do – they will absorb what you have done, enjoy glimpses of it – a painting here, a paragraph there – and go about their lives, with you being but a brief footnote in the story of their existence. There will be those who dislike you and avoid what you do, thinking you to be a fool, a liar, a jerk – someone whose very name brings about an unpleasant feeling - and they would no sooner be done for hearing it. And there will be those who despise you. Nothing you do will please them. They will hate you vehemently for your existence and everything you stand for. It is important to be aware of all these types in whatever you do and know that – for most – you will be a pleasant footnote and for some a little more and to leave it at that.

The Silence

Most who go through the process of creation – be it on screen or in book, will find that they will not be greeted with hordes of ravenous haters, foaming at the mouth and screeching from the highest rooftops for your end. Nor will you be met with throngs of crowds gathered to hear your word spill forth like you are a fountain from heaven. You won't even be seen by those who mildly like or dislike you. No, unless you already have some renown about you – of which most of us do not fall into this category – you will be met with silence. Pure and utter silence. A constant and deafening scream of silence. There will be no fanfare. No anger, nor love. Nothing. Simply silence. In some ways it could be said to be worse. You will not know if what you have made had any effect or relevance. It will feel like your works never existed at all. The silence can ruin many men and it is important to be painfully aware of it. There will be nothing, and for it you must be ready. See your work as a long, painful and lonely trek through a long desert expanse where nothing will greet you and – if you are fortunate, one day you may find your oasis. Do not expect instead, that your journey will be constantly encroached upon by a river, and that you can drink greatly and readily – for any such fool will quickly die of thirst.

On Writing

You must write. You must write that which you think and feel. It is necessary. Write for yourself, for the betterment of yourself. And what if you do not want to write for the betterment of yourself? Write for someone you care about, and wish to share with them the lessons you have learned about life and this world – like that of your child – should you be dead and gone tomorrow. And what if you do not have a child? Then write as if you write for your future child. What if you never want children? Then write for someone you care deeply about. What if you care for no one? Then write for a society that you feel would be ever the better for having heard of your wisdom. But what if you don't want to help yourself, your child, your future children, your loved ones or society? Then rot, and the world would have been better without knowing of your thoughts.

Truth & Lies

There is but only one way to tell the truth of a thing, but there is a vast infinity of lies that could be said about it. Truth is concrete, absolute. Lies are countless, they can expand greatly based upon the ability of the liar who weaves them. A truth is universal, it is better having been discovered. A lie is chaotic, if the world was built upon nothing but lies, we would find ourselves in the depths of anarchy. Truths are what we strive for to make the world a better place. Lies are the chaos we sow when we wish to spread disarray. But be wary – if you find yourself to be a truth-teller – for the world is filled with liars. If you wish to exist within this world, you do

so under the awareness that the world is deeply competitive, and that –
while you may speak truths many others do not. Truths are usually
humble; they are small and insignificant most of the time. They are just,
and sometimes they are boring. They are explainable and rational and all
too sensible. A lie is alluring, a lie can be told to benefit that of the listener,
whereas if a listener benefits from a truth told that is merely convenience.
You apply for a job, and there are discrepancies in your resume, what have
you been doing during this time? Where have you been? Helping your sick
loved one. Spending that time studying for yourself in an autodidact
manner, even if you may not have the credentials to show for it. Noble,
but not what they want to hear. And you, truth-teller, are all the worse for
it. What of the liar, what fantastical tales can he spin to an employer to
make their absence all the more exciting and explainable? What noble
pursuits, exciting adventures and relevant skills can they weave to a
member of corporate, a colleague or even a potential love interest? The
noble and righteous truth-teller must then ask himself the question, if I
live in an ever-competing world then I go against my peers, and that, in
this world there are many of them who would lie willingly and regularly,
and I am at a disadvantage for it. A good liar is one who is not caught. A
good liar is one who can make others believe in the words they spin. It
makes sense then, that a good liar can best both the bad liars and the
truth-tellers, for bad liars will be caught out and truth-tellers will almost
always never live up to a carefully crafted series of lies. What does this
mean for you or I, if you are one who prefers to speak truth? Spill your

truths freely and often to those close to you or whom you see in a positive manner, but be ready to bare the weapons of lies should there be a time that they are needed, for without doing so you will be at a devastating loss. Or perhaps you could not live with yourself for doing such a thing.

Be Hated

You will never be your true, unrestricted self unless you face the fact that in order to do so you must be willing to bear the sting of others' bitter opinions. To be hated, is to voice oneself. If you are not hated, no one has seen you or you have played too safe in your words and said nothing at all. I would even go so far as to say that you should mention things at times that would intentionally make you hated by the masses, even broadcasting a video on the matter and be all the stronger for it. You hate this animal, you don't like this beloved person, you hate Saturdays, you hate this 'insert worthless consumer product/TV show/video game that the majority enjoy', all to prod and provoke the masses. You will face their hurtful words, their anger and fury – and make it through the other side, perfectly fine and intact. And through it all you will realise that no true harm was dealt to you. That the friends and family you love know you well and still care for you. That the words of the many never mattered, for they spend no time in your company and care not for you even one brief iota. That you have cast down the shackles of the masses opinion that shape who you are and what you can say, and now you have but a lighter burden that holds down your freedom (even if shackles still remain, like that of your loved ones' opinions and one's own fears, among others).

The Group has its Own Mind

When we talk to another person – once we have done away with shallow speech – we can peel back their layers and uncover their true self. Their thoughts, fears, aspirations, past lives, past loves, most things. But when we are introduced to a group, even one as small as an extra person, we no longer find ourselves in the company of another person. We find ourselves in the company of the group. The group is dynamic, it shifts based on the number of occupants within. It is as small as three people and as large as a horde. Peoples' personal identity is stripped away and paves the way for something else entirely. It is almost like a beast, one with its own form – held by the reigns of the most talkative members, while its limbs and features are composed by the masses of the silent. It moves by way of consensus. It speaks only in ways that hold court of popular opinion. It steers away from the controversial or the philosophical (unless in rare circumstances all the individual members are composed as such, or the reign-holders – the talkative ones – deem to steer the beast in that way, for but a moment). Many are terrified of the beast. Many choose never to take the reins at all when it is in their presence. Some, like to avoid it as much as possible. Some are simply struck in terror and fear when the beast turns its attention to the individual, such as on a stage or platform. With regards to public speaking and talking to large audiences, I have been told – although I don't often practice it – that in order to survive the beast one must strip down its layers. That ultimately, the beast is composed of many different members and that – in order to stave off its terror – should speak to the members as individuals, to pick them out, to ask questions, to bring forth the people who comprise it as just that – people. Once this is done can we start to understand we are not looking at some anonymous monster and make it out the other side all the better for it.

Anger

Anger is like that of a stream that spews upwards from a volcano. Once it happens there is no good that can be done to prevent it, only shame is felt afterwards from a regrettable action or sentence that cannot be undone. Once it has been felt, we must ask ourselves the reason why it happened? Why, truly? Has a person insulted you or your family? If this person doesn't matter to you or hold any relevance then what of it, they do not matter. Has a loved one angered you in some way? What have they done? Before this, ask what have you done. Have you slept enough, eaten enough, are you primed and ready for stress and anger after having much of your willpower drained from the strains of the day? What can you do differently in these matters? Why were all other days fine but not today, what was done differently? Anger is not to be tackled upon its happening, but rather prevented and avoided before it even comes about, and learned from afterwards when it comes to call. Better to find ways to calm and contain the bull, rather than investing in weapons once it comes to destroy our houses.

Waves of Censorship

We find ourselves faced with waves of censorship. Our true selves hidden behind layer-upon-layer of restricted thoughts, censored by humanity, culture, peers, groups, family, friends, loved ones, the self – all of which a thick and elaborate coating slick upon ourselves which we must peel off in order to tackle the next thought or action. Perhaps it is all the better that we have these layers, for without them we would pursue only for that of the self, and maybe resort to base instincts and chaos. But at the same time, it is important to realize that this coating which protects us at times, functions as restricted, sticky tar at others. If one ever finds themself thinking, "Can I do this?", "Can I say that?", "Can I think this?", then first question why. One must pull off these layers, sometimes at different depths, in order to pursue that past the self or society at large. That we will never be anything more if we cannot breach the surface of the ocean beneath all the overlapping waves of censorship that plunges upon us and pulls us down.

Pander to Idiots

With regards to fame, one should consider this a cardinal rule. From books, internet fame, television, media in general, one must remember that there are far more idiots than intelligents, if there was such a word. Think of the demographics which comprise the masses. Children are idiots, in that they simply haven't lived and learned enough from the world yet. Idiots are idiots. Even intelligent people can at times be idiots – how often have some brighter individuals chosen to "dumb down" their minds by watching trash television, or consuming worthless media in their spare time? Plenty. In that, it seems many can possess the mind of an idiot, but rarely does this concept roll uphill. Idiots do not wish to "smarten up" with educational, informative, life-altering information. They are happy to continue consuming emptily. So, it is always important to pander to idiots if you wish to cast the widest net, and then to hone your works later if you wish to attract those who simply had a brief moment of idiocy, or to let others catch your works when you are mounted upon renown. Humour is a great example of this. On YouTube, videos that exist purely for humour cast a wide net, garnering significant views. The most viewed ones are the simplest of all. A silly face and a childish joke can pull in a wide assortment of children, teenagers, fools and "intelligents" in a moment of foolishness, but a joke with context, a setup or punchline that needs to be first learned and understood alienates the widest of demographics. In a world where success and fame are made by being linked and shared with friends and family, talked about on podcasts, "retweeted", posted on forums, have reaction responses made about said content along with everything else in between – remember this rule and your creations will breed success – pander to idiots.

How to Achieve this Fame and Success

So how could such be done? How can one achieve this kind of fame and success? We are generally a species that values the negative over the positive and the worthless over the worthwhile. Why do I say such? First the negative. Man does not value the positive, not to the extent that his own life suffers from the success of others if he himself is in a negative position. We do not care for happy stories, they bore us so. A massacre or a plane crash will always gather far more attention from the news, simply because they know all too well that similar content about the children that have been adopted into a loving family or the creation of a life-changing technology that could help many will never be cared about, spoken of nor pursued with keen interest in any comparable way. The useless and the useful are much the same. Useful is boring. Useful takes hard work and determination to be learned upon. Useless is easy. Useless can be binged over and over again like that of a delicious snack with no nutritional value. Useless is what we watch after a long, hard day at work and have expunged all of our willpower. Useless is what "gets us throughout the day", while useful is "I don't have the energy for this". With this in mind, the content that one can create which would garner the most amount of success or fame can be considered to be negative and/or useless. The most sustaining and attention grabbing videos for the masses can generally be some of the following: reviews and criticisms of some sort of media (TV/books/video games/movies), negative criticisms of another person (generally considered some kind of "drama" between the two), entertainment in general (as useless), whereas the likes of education (useful) and charitable works (positive) can garner success when they can find a specific niche, but pale in comparison to the views and success of the former categories mentioned above. No educators will achieve the success and fame of an entertainer, barring outliers. Nor will empaths rival that of contrarians. Not that one should worry about such things if you seek to attain value and purpose, but it is important to remember it all the same.

The Colour or The Instrument

This day I have caught myself noting that at times my writings come about from an instance of an emotion one is feeling within the moment. Sometimes I find myself writing during moments of contentment, happiness, melancholia, depression, among others and yet I find myself wondering the question – if a man creates the same content, say, a bowl made from a mound of clay whilst feeling happiness, then tries to make the exact same on another day while feeling melancholic, how different would they look? Will the mould have differences or rather, would the potter wish to make something entirely different on that day? What of a philosopher? What questions open up to him when he stands in different avenues of emotions, or should he be faced with the same question and answer it all-to-differently? What true self could there be if that was such a thing, we would be like pieces of shattered glass, only being the self of the piece or emotion one is holding. What of a painter? Did Van Gogh create his works purely under certain feelings? Was each painting a different feeling or did he ever feel like painting only when he had a certain feeling?

What about a greater specificity? Was Michelangelo's Mona Lisa painted in patches of feelings: a hair strand under euphoria, the iris under depression, the complete canvas actually portraying a wider range of emotions encapsulated within? What I am saying, then, is are our emotions representative of a colour providing a slightly different shade upon the canvas (like answering the same question but giving different answers based on the mood), or is it more like that of an instrument – the sound of which simply cannot be played unless we are holding it. Can we ask a particular question or paint a particular painting when, and only when, we feel a specific emotion?

Elicit an Emotion

To create beautiful food is to elicit an emotion. To paint a beautiful picture is to elicit an emotion. To compose a wonderful musical piece is to elicit an emotion. To act superbly is to elicit an emotion. To be funny is to elicit an emotion. To write a fascinating tale is to elicit an emotion. To be a great entertainer is to elicit an emotion. To be a friend is to elicit an emotion. To be a lover is to elicit an emotion.

Don't be Too Serious

Don't take life too seriously. Life can be a miserable, gruelling haul. A struggle to exist amongst the noise and desperate clamouring of competition pulling one down so they can be on top. It is a world of death, decay and suffering. But we already know all of that. To live is to laugh in its face. We are creatures of ego. We take ourselves very seriously in how we portray ourselves to others – the strangers and the familiars. We reinforce ourselves by our attitudes and dispositions in our general lives. We fear and worry about the consequence of acting a fool, making a distasteful joke or making our appearance altered in a way that isn't carefully controlled or choreographed for the latest visual social media. Beware of this, to release it all is in some ways a kind of freedom. To remove the confines of who we show ourselves to be – pushed down by the harsh realities of the world and let the inner child step in. The child within does not care. They care not for the image, nor ego, nor consequence. They wish for the happiness and foolishness of the present moment. If you are a sort who takes themselves too seriously, know the ego of oneself holds you in place. Act a fool, do a silly dance in front of others, make jokes, the child will thank you for it while the ego will squirm and ask why you did such a silly thing at all.

What Others Want

Sometimes we must face the cold, hard truth that what we value and wish to dedicate ourselves to – possibly a passion – can be seen as utterly valueless in the eyes of others. To avoid the perils of becoming a "starving artist", we must look towards an overlapping diagram of two things, do we enjoy it, yes, but also do others find a worth in it too. Is what you are selling unique and special, or could it be found by many others, plentifully, at better cost or in a well-established environment? If you choose to pursue your interest regardless of others, know that it is a hobby, and no fame nor fortune will come of it. Do not look upon it bitterly, that it does not put food in your belly or provide you with finer things, as in doing so it will become tainted and you will lose your passion for it as such. If others enjoy what you do then a career may be viable, after long hard work and determination, along with some luck. Sometimes one may be faced with the grueling possibility that what one provides may even be for the greater good and that it is genuinely useful for others, but they may not care for it. It is ultimately up to them to decide its value. Then one must face themselves with the question, after long and hard silences, if that, what one pursues is their work or their hobby.

Mood

Sometimes a mood is fleeting. It is the ever-constant waiting to be in the right mindset for something. Sometimes we wait for this mood to strike us, waiting days, weeks, even months before it allows itself to be known. Sometimes it is necessary for it instead to be forced. How often a mood strikes when one does not feel ready to step outside and go for a run, to go to a gym and pull a weight towards one's body or to pick up a pen and start writing. Sometimes we must do so regardless, and in the very act of doing so does the mood on occasion become roused. Sometimes does the mood then follow. Sometimes, often times, do we allow our moods to dictate our actions, rather than its reverse. For a scheduled life does this drill home the point that we should not simply be the result of a mood in a fleeting moment but a consequence of the actions chosen that shapes our path, and resist the temptations of it being something all too otherwise chaotic.

The Mind & The Body

The mind and the body are inextricably linked. I would say that the mind is the body, or rather a facet of it. This is clear when we think of how consequential the result of the body is when influenced by the thought of the mind. Think of a fear, perhaps a fear of a social encounter or an anxiety. What happens to the body is an evident linking of the pair. The fearful thoughts cause rapid heartbeats, sweat across the skin, increased and exaggerated breathing of the lungs and a variety of other ailments that would not present themselves outside of this stressful encounter. What if we take another example of the inverse? Much is said about trying to alter the body in order to influence the thoughts of the mind. Focused breathing can help in times of stressful situations. Meditation can balm a racing mind. Exercise can convert the thoughts of a lazy and idle mind after extended periods of time. They are like two partners of the same relationship, where each one will influence the other. Even our very thoughts can only occur through the influence of our body. What thoughts will one have without the senses to learn and perceive from? Take your eyes away, then learn through sound. Take your ears, learn in Braille. Take your touch, taste, smell, what have you left to interact with the world and create thoughts for the mind? The senses are the tools we use in the sandbox of thought. We need the body to breathe in thoughts for the mind like we need lungs to breathe in the very air. If the mind is not desperately linked with the body, then let us ask what the mind thinks once we take the body away, ha! Perhaps one of the underlying reasons why some consider the mind to be separate from the body is they conflate the concept of the mind with that of the soul and that to take the soul out of someone is to take their thoughts, knowledge and experiences out of them. But then wouldn't that be the mind? Do we take our brains with us when we die (like that of a ghost brain), or is even the mind left behind and is the soul an utterly blank slate? What makes it unique or special then? Is there even such a thing?

Wisdom from a Hawk

There is danger to wisdom. That which applies to one, may rarely apply to another. We all hold different lives, different positions of status, different health and ailments, with completely separate views of the world based on our values and disinterests. Our friends, social groups, intelligence, outside influences based on an ever-shifting technological presence - are all too different. To hear wisdom from one is like listening to the wisdom of a hawk when we are but an octopus, or a horse. A field mouse, cat, dog, what difference. Listen to the great words he speaks, born from observation and experience, how he learns to navigate the world, the optimum way he catches his prey, how he deals with potential threats. All well and all true, for the hawk. What worth to you? Perhaps there is some overlap. We all have our basic needs that should be looked after. To sleep, eat and exercise. Global wisdom may be found within those, for we all need. But wisdom for everything else must be heeded cautiously, for what is wise for one may be worthless to another.

Death

On the concept of death, it is but a great equalizer. All of the money made, knowledge gained, the friends and family crafted along the way, none of it can be taken with us. Unless the ancient Egyptians had it right and you can take all of that with you, but if death was that demonstrably unbalanced one would hope there would be quite an uproar from all the masses being treated unfairly in the hereafter. But then again, it would be rather apt that the unfairness of existence be carried over to that in the afterlife also, but alas – one thinks that death is equal in all things. In some ways, I find it to be reassuring that all which was handed out in life, a lottery of sorts in many aspects – genetic, family and fortune – can all return to its null and void state. What then, does it end, continue or restart once we reach the point of expiry? For it to simply end bothers me not, for it will return to how it was before birth, a sense of non-existence. To be sad about such is only to be sad in the present living moment, for during all feelings will be gone. Sad for what has been lost in all the earnings made of this existence, but what of it if it is such an unavoidability? What then for an existence that continues after death? This one I find to be the most worrisome of all. In what capacity? I can comprehend a restart of an existence or a complete ending of one (like imaging another person's life or how one remembers nothing of a long, dreamless slumber), but what experience do we have of an eternity? What

107

experiences do we have of infinity? In a finite amount of lived years through the senses how am I to comprehend existence where all senses are removed and one is faced with a realm where time has no meaning? And what of the realm itself? Is it a reflection of this one, riddled with its consumptions and vices? Is it some childlike fantasy cloud land, cherry-picked from the latest in popular religion? Is it whatever you imagine in one's wildest, fantasy dreams like a magical genie land? How much control does one wield within it? Is this realm utterly alien in its concept that we cannot possibly envision it? It is all too perplexing. And what of the people who preach these religious texts – the shamans, druids, priests and a whole host of others. What do they know, for them and I have in equal the same number of deaths, and we shall all find out the answer in much the same way. Of all three conclusions I think I would prefer the repeating / reincarnation, as it were, and would close this segment by comparing it to a video game. I would much rather play a video game where each time one starts a new game has a whole new selection of skills, traits and possibilities to collect and choose from, rather than complete a game to its conclusions, having amassed everything that can be obtained from it but having to continue playing anyway.

Philosophy

Philosophy is available to all, for those who wish to use it. It is not to be gate kept – hidden behind tomes, rules, and regulations – only for the stuffy professors, crusty wizened archetypes, or philosophical greats that you may have heard about in books that lived all those years ago. Those who can think can philosophize. Those who can think, must philosophize. As freely as one can write, one can think. Think often and question everything. Wonder about everything and our place in this world. Philosophy is not just reserved for universities, waiting for the consensus of the masses, it is for oneself, and the picture he can paint upon the canvas of his mind can be as unique and beautiful as any artist – working with the paintbrushes of one's own knowledge and experiences.

Has philosophy suffered in this time? No modern-day greats will ever bring forth the masses to hear their words, like we line up in our droves for sports players, comedians, or celebrities. Did we ever? Is modern philosophy shrivelled when compared to the days of ancient Greek philosophers, or has the majority never cared for it, never cared to think more about themselves or past themselves? To never think past more than the current, fleeting moments of life – that would be a great shame.

The Virtual Machine

Imagine a device that can show you anything you wish to see. Not only this, but an audience of other human beings who also agree and reinforce that same thing you are viewing. They may even cite hand-packed evidence that corresponds with that particular view, incite anecdotal evidence or reinforce it with emotional or logical reasoning. After viewing this particular ideology, you are then recommended similar content. Over and over, you are given an ever-inflated perception of what you believe, not necessarily anchored in reality. This is the internet. A magical and mysterious world that is exclusively based in fantasy. Its illusions are based in nothing but a warped reality, eco-chambers, survivorship biases, confirmation fallacies and - ultimately - those whose content you consume is only done with an ulterior motive of capturing and retaining audiences for a larger subscriber base or view count, inevitably to garner financial success, fame and/or attention. Yet despite all of this, the power of the internet grows ever stronger. More and more people find themselves trapped in longer hours of binge-watching and mindless scrolling. More people find themselves losing vast swaths of hours only to look back and reflect afterwards on how little the past few hours had meant to them. How valuable and worthwhile it hadn't been and what little worth it had been for them. The long-term, unexamined and empty compulsion of internet use will one day be looked back upon as the 21st century equivalent to smoking. A fundamental drain on those who use it, only diminishing their health and resulting in a net loss, particularly to those who binge and excess. How can one tell the truth in an environment where ideologies are praised by the many, regardless of how ridiculous? How can one tell the true price of success when you are in an environment where that is all that is ever shown and the hordes of failures stay silent in the darkness? Failure can never attain the view counts of success, after all. If you engage in acts, no matter how foolish and destructive, but are surrounded by similar like-minded fools, how can you ever see your doom? The net is a world that desperately seeks attention for personal profit, people clamour for tribal identity based on tautologies, is deeply shallow to the extent of the individual, and revels in the uncanny valley of creating what many are fooled into believing is reality when all is fantasy.

The Few & The Many

Throughout much of life it is important to remember a vital rule - that the few are responsible for the many and the many are responsible for the few. Take strawberry plants. Go to a wide field where there are many and walk around examining the plants. Take note that some will have only one or a couple of strawberries, while others are barren. Others still will have several berries, some berries will even be huge in size compared to other yields. Take the stock market next. When we look at the highest ranking stocks we can see that it is only the few that reap the profits, yet covers the loss of the many that make nothing, while the rest simply break even. Women too, talk to many and the same principle applies. Most will do nothing, but end conversations quickly, showing little interest, while others will be a little more courteous, yet equally as fruitless. Then there are the small few who would end up as significant chapters in one's own life, spending many years in your company and providing the largest returns in shared experiences. The few being responsible for the many and the many being responsible for the few. The minority and the majority. This is known as the Pareto Principle, and you may notice its effects much throughout life like I. In that small, seemingly minor choices in life can end up being the pathway to huge and significant changes later on, "I'll talk to this person", "I'll go here", "I'll make this decision", leading to drastic changes that alter the path of your existence. Even in sales, we don't look at the thousands of failed emails and calls that result in nothing, but rather the handful that can net thousands. Even reading books I have noticed the principle. It's not in the hundreds and hundreds of words that are eye-opening, but in only a few sentences here and there that truly define a book and make it remarkable. Movies too have their scenes that are tense and remarkable that stand out and define the film, even if the majority of it is rather drool and boring. I could go on, but I won't.

Good Tech, Bad Tech

In the 21st century we are inundated with what I would consider to be bad technology, as far as the internet is concerned. This technology has only been used by the majority of the populous for no more than a decade or so. As such, we are currently in an era where there is no regard for the internet user. No care for their safety or mental health. Humans are only commodified in this regard, treated only as a consumer, waiting to extract their wallet - be it from purchasing products, advertisements shown to them or them "willingly" giving money through parasocial relationships and parasitic websites like OnlyFans. Ideally, this century will hopefully shift to one where technology can be used for the better. Where videos can help and convey truth without misleading information and monetary incentive in mind. Where relationships with others aren't built in empty, shallow, one-sentenced communication with strangers and form parasocial relationships with others, but instead can be fostered with care, depth and the ability to meet others locally face-to-face instead of never meeting at all. One day perhaps because of the false identities people use online we will cast these aside to show ourselves and step away from fantasy and better harness our reality. The more I write this the less likely I can see it happening. One can only hope there are more positive instances of internet technology in the future. This could include allowing people to meet others in offline environments face-to-face instead of on computer screens. Rewarding and incentivising others to do more volunteering and charity works. A better integration and community fostering of physical exercise, making it a part of some communal internet activities, instead of always being stagnant when using it. We could build better algorithms that instead of trying to keep you retained on a platform, showing you ultimately meaningless dribble, could be used to help you find hobbies or activities you may never have even considered. Only time will tell if we start to transition into good tech, as the internet is currently in its adolescence.

A Note on Insignificance

You exist in but a tiny, inconsequential sliver of time on a rock cast about on an endless void of nothingness. This rock, too, a worthless speck. Your time while living will be spent pursuing tasks that have no bearing or meaning amongst people who will be dead and gone in nothing more than the blink of an eye. Your life will be forgotten quickly after death. Only fractions of segments of memories from those who remember you, which they too will forget after a handful of years or so, just before they too become bones. Books and inventions and buildings and memories all crumble and fade away over time, replaced with the next or with dust.

Everything that was believed in will be gone. Everything you have or hold dear will be gone. Remember this when you cling to petty things like your own ego or possessions. They mean nothing. You mean nothing. Take time to dwell on your own insignificance.

3 Questions to Determine Someone's Worth

It is important to determine the quality of those around you to consider those of whom are truly on your side when compared with those who are simply using you for attention. These three questions you should ask when thinking of an individual are: Will they attend your birthday, will they visit you when you have a serious illness in the hospital, will they attend your funeral. With these 3 questions posed on any individual, you can determine the quality of their relationship with you at any given time. The questions you yourself pose may differ, but these three cover important broader aspects of a person's character. Will they share with you in joyous times (the birthday), will they be there in times of your suffering (injured in hospital), will they be there at the end (funeral). Of all three the second question is the most important. Who is there under grievous injury, under heartbreak and suffering. Who is there when your home burns down or when your misery is the greatest. Who is there when you yourself are not as you should be, such as when recovering from a crippling drug or medication. The third question is more subjective, as we cannot truly know who will be there at the end, nor does it help to determine who is there for you or who is there simply to keep up appearances for others. Also those who don't show up may grieve in their own way, choosing to discard the empty appearances of a funeral. As such this question isn't so important, but it does help set the focus in the right direction, to reflect on our own mortality. That one day we shall be nothing more than bones and dust. Who weeps for me today when I am gone? Is there anyone? Knowing that our story will end and who are the characters left behind is a useful one to dwell on. Finally the first question, you will find those who wish to soak in and share in your happiness. You will find friends with these, but if they do not show up in times of suffering you will only have surface level friends / fair weather friends - those who show up for the good times and disappear during the bad. Now to test these questions you must think of an individual and run them through the gauntlet of the 3 Questions. If you get zero then this person is either a new acquaintance or this person should be meaningless to you, as they see you as worthless to them. If they get one right they are a developing friend or a surface level friend. If they get two they are likely a good friend or close family. If you get three cherish them as they do for you.

More Valuable than Money

In this consumptionist-era in which we live, as we look around and see that many of those around us desperately try to pursue and obtain money, wanting more and not satisfied with enough. Driving expensive cars, wearing expensive clothes and jewellery and craving the latest expensive tech. It's important to ask "Is this all there is?", and wonder if wealth is the pinnacle of man's achievement. I believe that there are things far more important than money and will illustrate some of the following. My simple criteria is that if I had vast wealth but didn't have the following then life would be miserable. That is not to say you cant have these things and wealth, you can of course - that would be nice - but simply money is not the ultimate gain nor achievement. In fact, I would wager most rich individuals would desperately divert a sizable portion of their income to attain some or all of these. First I wish to talk about health - both physical and mental. Health is one of the core, primary tenants of life but because most of us are born with it in good condition we take it for granted. We abuse it, we eat like shit and don't move our bodies, we riddle ourselves with alcohol and narcotics for brief spikes of pleasure only to chip away at something sacred - our physical and mental condition. Anyone who has experienced a crippling health condition knows how it ruins our ability to live. Not even live well, but simply to live, as the pain renders us incapable of even the simplest of tasks. Some mental conditions can be so debilitating that it even robs us of our ability to remember our loved ones or even ourselves. I'm sure any rich tycoon would give all they have to remove Alzeimers, or cancer, or a crippling physical illness. Some fools make their wealth yet end up getting fat and slow. Regardless of one's finances, never neglect your health. Exercise regularly, eat natural, un-processed foods most - if not - all of the time, since nutrition is linked to many cancers and physical / mental diseases. Doing this, one's quality of life will improve significantly. Another important value is quality relationships - be it friends or family. Those who you can be with and share in the good times and bad. Those who you have crafted experiences with together. Who you have learned from and grown together with. Those who have wealth but no good quality relationships shall have a miserable and empty existence if they cannot remedy this. They may in a sense be trapped, as they feel that those around them are simply using them for money. It is best to find and create these relationships by crafting good-quality shared experiences. Go out with people, try new things. Over time some relationships will harden while others fall to the wayside. Another is education. Learning is growth. Without growth there is stagnation. Pursue that which interests you and discover the world. Libraries are goldmines - educationally speaking of course. Learn, grow and live. Although it is quite rare for the wealthy to avoid education, usually they are the first to embrace it, and will throw whatever the cost is to learn - as some knowledge and pathways are opened up faster in this world of money. By educating ourselves we can learn about our health, we can communicate with each other better, we can learn from masters in their field throughout the course of history and learn from perspectives we would have never encountered otherwise. Another which can be often overlooked is experiences. Money is indifferent to experiences. They can be bought or the money can sit in a bank, never to be touched. Either way, the point and purpose of life's greatest moments are that of experiences. They can involve travelling to a new country, learning or trying something different, meeting another person. Something novel. In this way we can live in an ever-constant state of flux, and without it life becomes stagnant.

These four things: health, good relationships, education and experiences are worth their weight in gold.

Most People

Most people do not read. Most people do not exercise or take care of their health. Most people eat junk food. Most people spend eight hours of their lives daily working a job they dislike or don't love. Most people take some form of drug (alcohol, weed, smoking cigarettes). Most people spend money on worthless shit that doesn't matter. Most people think a good time is living in a zombie-like state five days a week then living for the weekend by consuming alcohol and throwing money away going to clubs and bars. Most people dress like shit. Most people look like shit. Most people use social media. Most people bumble around not knowing who to be or what to do with their lives. Most people think education ends after school. Most people care about the opinions of others who don't matter. Most people think they matter. Most people think they are good when really they have accomplished no good deeds and are simply harmless. Most people don't think for themselves. Most people think they are the movies, shows and music they spend an agonizing part of their lives consuming. Most people don't write. Most people don't travel past what they have always known. Most people don't reflect. Most people don't grow. I think it's best to avoid being like most people.

How Modern Living Causes Greater Individuality

Take one thousand years ago. Life was simple and moved slowly. You would know those in your town or village around you. There was little to no growth, be it educational, technological or financial. Even the growth of buildings was slow and built to last. Contrast with now, the rate of change has skyrocketed. The difference between a fathers life and even his own sons is radically different. Look at the growth of technology in this span, like the internet, smartphones, speed, ability and capacity of technological devices. Look at how easily globalization has come about thanks to cheaper airline costs. Look at the rise of Artificial Intelligence. At how college education is considered the societal norm. How cultures are able to spread and multiply across the globe like has never been seen before. How people no longer depend on a tribe or village in a geographical location of dozens or hundreds in a community but now live in cities of millions of complete and abject strangers. This radical shift in living and circumstance has brought about wide, sweeping individual change. No longer do we know the same people our entire lives but now they alter and change, as we move about and as do they. No longer do we live in a time of technological stagnation but now it moves so fast even looking back a decade seems alien. No longer do we toil on a field or profession that our family has done for generations but must now choose between countless thousands, and have to keep up with the latest accreditations and certifications. Is there any wonder there is wide sweeping loneliness, brought about by rapid and constant change. Where people, buildings, economy, technology, professions, fields and possibilities are in a constant state of flux. All of these hoisted upon any person causes a shattering and splintering of the self resulting in a greater sense of individuality.

A Yearning for Shared Experience through Media

It is perhaps because of this shattering of any real shared experience with others that the modern person tries to seek out shared experiences in strange and bizarre ways. Instead of sharing physical events together "Do you remember when we had that storm?", "I heard Jerry got sick, what happened?". People clutch to artificial experiences that are syndicated, like "Did you watch the latest - whatever - movie?", "What do you think of - whoever's - new song?", "I cant believe that happened in - who cares". Fake experiences created by corporations to elicit emotion and foster artificial shared encounters. Instead of depth it creates shallowness, since the price of admission is easy. Simply pay the price of the consumerist media. Now people are riddled with these fake experiences that they will actually judge others for not sharing in them. "I cant believe he doesn't watch X", "What music do you like?", "What's your favourite TV show?". All shallow artificially created experiences. No depth. Nothing about the person themselves. What do they get up for? What brings them joy? What do they create and not consume?

The Tale of Two Badgers

Once upon a time there were two badgers, a father badger and a son badger, who lived together in a burrow deep beneath the ground under a rich and beautiful forest. Every day the father badger would travel above ground, to the ripe forest and find some delicious food for him and his son to share. Tasty berries from the bushes, succulent earthworms in the fertile soil and birds in nearby nests. As the years passed the father badger had become old and it was time for his son to take his place and find food for them. However as time passed this was not all that had changed. Man had travelled through this forest and what was ripe and lush was now black, barren and desolate from fires, hunting, deforestation and the like. The son would travel above to go hunting but his father had been underground for some time now. Every time the son had returned with nothing to feed them the father would try his best to help his son with advice. "This is the best time to search the soil for worms" he would say, or "You must search the second lowest branch on the pine trees, there you will find the birds nests!". The son would try to tell his father the folly of his advice, but he would not listen and they starved some time after. The lesson: Sometimes the advice of even our closest loved ones can be empty, for our environment has irrevocably changed from what they once knew.

Competition for the 21st Century Man

Today's man is beset from all angles against fierce competition in the job market. Some of which I wish to highlight now. Machines/Algorithms - While man's competition with machinery is nothing new, there is however a pivotal difference. When new technology came about it was still expected that man would be required to operate them. This is now no longer the case. The man has now been replaced by algorithms and computer software. Think how self-checkouts have replaced human cashiers, or how the upcoming driverless car revolution will make human drivers utterly obsolete, already drivers being a significant portion of jobs on the market. In the past, staff could be trained to operate these machines but now they are no longer needed. The technical skill required as an engineer makes it unattainable for most and besides, significantly less are needed for upkeep and maintenance. So I ask, where does man turn? Next I refer to the best in their respective fields. The talented. The exceptional. Thanks to increased competition from the fact that more people attend college now more than ever but also how competition has grown thanks to globalization, we see a staggering increase in those who apply for the same job. What was once a battle against others in one's geological approximation is now on the scale of ability - worse, equal and better than you, across the globe. And with so many doing what you do the chances of a significant portion of people being better than you and more likely to get the job is high. Another similar vein thanks to globalization is who can do it cheaper than you - the race to the bottom. Since many jobs don't particularly need an experienced specialist and everyone can produce similar results it therefore becomes who can do it at a lower price. Where those who live on lower income continents can find an acceptable wage while others are jostled out of the market. Another are corpses. Some fields hold experts whose talent lies in their ability to produce something distinct. Think of artists. The music, painting, or book doesn't build on itself in a technical capacity, it simply is and does not need to be expanded upon. Once an artist is dead that piece of work still lives on. How many music sales are made where the artist is now dead, I wonder? How many books? As long as we have the medium to capture and contain our talents, the dead will be in competition with us. How many starving artists busk for pennies on the street while we are happy to listen to a recording of the dead? How many writers? This too falls into the previous source of competition - the talent, just slightly altered since we don't reflect on the talented dead. As time passes this will only rise. As we have the mediums to capture and record others better now more than ever.

Machines/algorithms, the talented, the cheap and the dead are just some sources of competition in most fields.

Thoughts

Thoughts are a strange business. They are a vital and core component of who we are, what we stand for, and what we do in our lives and yet, they are also nothing at all. They can't be seen, nor have any tangible place in our world, yet they consume us. We are riddled with ideas of hope, belief, ideologies all paved and defined when the hammer of emotions strike the weapon of experience. And still, thoughts can run away from us. They can grow far bigger than what actually exists in the real lived and shared world, and guide us down a path of delusion. They can also lead us down a path or track of thoughts, where one idea proceeds the next and the next and so on, trapping us in enclosed ideas. We don't move randomly about a field of different concepts, we stack upon our own existing ideologies. That perhaps is also why meditation is useful for thought. Thoughts are constant. Close your eyes and try to think of nothing at all, it cannot be done. Only for a few seconds, only perhaps the monks can try for a little longer. The mind quickly grasps at memories, at moments, ideas and fantasy. On futures and pasts that could be and could have been. All of it, noise and nothing more. Most of it has no relevance at this moment in time and yet we dwell on them. Some so much that they affect how we live presently. Try to silence the thoughts at times. Develop the ability to keep the mind silent in moments. For thoughts, while they can guide our principles and give us reasons for waking, can also overwhelm us.

On Finding the Perfect Job

Employment is a significant and unavoidable part of most people's lives. And yet a significant portion of us find ourselves with jobs we don't like. They are stressful, meaningless, disconnected from the tangibility of having done something worthwhile in the real world. They are droll, thankless and easily replaceable with another person. The modern man finds himself with an intangible question, "Is there a perfect job for me?". Is this a possibility? Is there more than one job or is there only one ideal and perfect job that you could fit into and all else forever would not live up to the task? What if your perfect job has now passed on, made irrelevant due to the current era you live in. What if your perfect job was a slinger or warrior, made redundant in the current era. Or a poet, back when it was viable to earn a living. Gone now, completely out of one's control. I cannot believe that there is but one and only one perfect job, and that due to circumstances beyond our control we could miss them forever. I believe there are traits, some based on the individual and others based on widespread human desires that lead to the conclusion of an ideal subset of jobs. First I want to discuss broader principles then drill down to individual specifics. First of man, and of our general desires in the world. We want meaning, we want whatever we do to have a tangible and realized effect on the world, we want what we do to have an impact on others and we want to feel special in some form. Many jobs now, including some of my own in the past, have lacked many of these basic principles. Many have involved sitting in a cubicle, doing work far removed from any tangible and important change in the world. Most jobs have also been so compartmentalized that an individual is only responsible for a small part of the overall result, and that the individual can be removed and replaced at a moment's notice, like a small defective component of a larger machine. We have also created "middle jobs", where we not only have the desire for something (A) and the final result (B), we now have the distribution, customer services, managerial factors, etc. to consider, creating an A, B, C, D, etc. pattern. These middle jobs can involve moving a piece of material from one warehouse to another in a chain (you being piece E and F), and not seeing anything of the tangible result. Concluding in an individual feeling completely disconnected in the process. Meaningless and redundant. So what would be a more rewarding job?

125

One where we can derive meaning, that what we do matters, that it has an impact on others and that the results can be felt in some real and tangible way. These are good fundamentals to draw upon in a general setting, but what about on an individual level? For example, when we look at the broad statement of "That what we do has an impact on others", who are the others? Based on the individual this can range from immediate loved ones like partners and children to a wider range like family, friends, community, tribe, region, nation, ideologues, world or specific species and subspecies. What we do having some kind of meaning or matter too would be based on the individual. What about scientific research? What of humour? What of entrepreneurship? What of health? Redundancy and subjectivity can be found in many instances of individual worth and meaning. How much can an individual handle stress? What is the individual's perception of money? What is the intelligence of this person, does it challenge them or bore them? How willing are they to face danger or put their lives on the line? Police, firefighters. Or are mentally capable of enduring horrific scenarios? Doctors, detectives, negotiators. How hungry do they yearn for fame or care for moving about in an ever-shifting environment? How connected do they wish to be with others in their daily lives? Little, like a programmer or constant turnover like a nurse or the wide range in between. When we look at the case of an individual level we can see there is much difficulty in finding an answer - if ever - and the more general questions should at the least function as a guiding star. Employment is one of these fields in a person's life that has the unfortunate position of being something which we have a large chance of getting wrong, but also of requiring so much time to invest in that we only have a few tries of getting it right.

A Reflection on Nature

The natural world is becoming a rarity in the eyes of the modern 21st century city-dwelling man. In his isolationist life it is already difficult for him to step outside of his own front door and yet even when he does, all that he will cast his eyes upon has been engineered by man. The placement of the trees and grass. The arrangements of the flowers chosen for which pleases the eye of man the most. Nature, in its untouched variety, has been pushed back into boundaries, behind borders known as "national parks and forests". Even parks, placating in its form of nature, have their grasses mown and hedges trimmed. Man's supposition of nature as we understand it now, is the greenery that has fallen under man's rule and order as most of us see it now. The land that is untamed and unmolested by man is a wild, chaotic and competitive place, a place most will rarely ever see yet connected by a primal, ape-nature we will always possess a yearning to return to. In nature, man feels a piece of the world. A small and inconsequential drop in a vast order of global life. It is a place teeming with life - the trees, animals, birds and insects, buzzing and chirping about aplenty. It is chaotic, like the largest of metropolises, yet still and calm, framed by the quiet of the trees that litter its place. In it, man is not the epicenter that he himself believes him to be but more like an inconsequential piece. That the birds, trees and insects would remain if not for him. And yet we push ourselves away from such a fact. Usher in generations of man never being out and one with nature. Never learning a fundamental part of our existence only to spend all of our age surrounded by man and only all of our own creations. How self-absorbed man is!

An Observation of Man

Man is a being that constantly struggles with being by itself. An antiquated ape, riddled with anxieties, illnesses, hope, wants and delusions that keeps its mind constantly smashing against itself. And so we fall into distracting ourselves to keep all of this noise at bay. A mind not distracted eventually succumbs to the noise and eventually kills itself or is driven mad. Therefore everything man does is a way for it to silence the noise of itself, if even it replaces the noise with more noise, albeit a significantly lower level. Why worry about existence or one's place in the world when one can worry about what will happen to some make-believe character in a pretend fantasy TV show? When the nature of the universe, how we fit into it or even what our own possible grim futures will look like we choose to replace the noise with another, to save the thoughts for another day or - like most - never have to think about them. If man truly had the ability to see his own life dozens of years into the future when you strip away the hope of potential and the mindless distractions of daily life and showed - without doubt - what they would inevitably become I am certain most would wish to die on the spot.

A Child is the Greatest Test of Man

A child is most assuredly the greatest test of man. In order to raise one of any success takes the greatest of one's endurance and mental faculties. All of a man's abilities are thrown back in his face during the course of child rearing and any such failures are shown in the unavoidable spotlight for him to see. Any addictions the man will have, the man will have to grapple with the fact he may pass the same to his child. Any social anxiety or lack of friends will also be passed down. The family or his lack of positive relationships with them will too be felt in the empty presence of would-be family members, who could have been there to help ease the burden of child rearing. When the child comes to the man will they be met with patience and kindness, or irritation and a fist? How does man cope when he is deprived of sleep, of solitude, of intellectual conversation and stimulation? It is the child of man unlike anyone else - not partner, parent, friend or the like that is so inexorably linked like the self to the child, as partners, strangers and friends come and go in their chapters, but the child is a reflection of the self, and all its success and failures, when undergoing constant and continuous periods of many years together and how one fares in the process.

On the Shallowness of the Internet

When I refer to the internet, I talk of a particular branch of it, namely social media, chat rooms and texting, the "social" aspects of the internet primarily. They make me laugh at how much of a pale imitation they are. Think for a moment how much of a social creature we are. How, over the course of many hundreds of thousands of years we developed, learned to work together as tribes, how we communicated through tone, facial expressions and body language - all for it to fall apart by staring at words on a screen. No context, no cues, no tonality, no expressions with the face - nor body - nothing. Is it any wonder there is so much misunderstanding through words on a screen? Take as another example video communication on a platform like YouTube. The uploader speaks some words all for a period of time, from minutes to hours, totalling thousands of words said. The viewer may leave a comment - equally likely is they say nothing at all - but say they comment, it is only a word, sentence or a paragraph long, totalling only a few dozen words at most by comparison. Thousands of words said one way, dozens said the other - how utterly unnatural a conversation. And then, the viewer is nothing but a literal and complete stranger, how unnatural this too, where the viewer looks more fondly at the person they are watching over time while the uploader does not know nor care to know of their existence. This one way social development - the parasocial. The thumbs up on videos and picture platforms - the comments - all of it utterly hollow and shallow. Nothing of the person themselves, nothing of their lived experiences - the individual - just something that supports or does not support the particular topic of whatever vapid subject. No comforting them when a loved one has passed, no touch or look or smile, no shared lived experiences. Nothing but an empty and fleeting transaction. To call "social media" on the internet as anything close to social is the same level of lunacy as comparing traveling

130

to the moon the same as looking at a picture of one. One is the real thing, while the other is nothing more than an empty and pathetic approximation.

A Snapshot of Modern Living

It is important to provide an introspective look on man - his daily struggles and monotony of existence. Modern man is raised believing he can be anything he wants to be. Can get anything he wants to get and do what he wants to do, provided one conforms to a harsh and gruelling grind to get there. Man surrounds himself in fantasy, from the constant bombardment of TV shows, movies, books, and other media, he believes he can do much should he work hard enough. Modern man is cast about in a godless and community-void world, where the only thing worshipped is not his character but the money he makes. Where the world has turned empty and unless one was fortunate to possess loving relationships, is cursed to roam about in a hollow world. Modern man exists in a world where the latest, expensive cars are bumper to bumper against shitty run-down ones, just one bad day away from breaking down. Where one of the latter could scratch one of the former and a man is ruined for life. Modern man is forced to work to the bone, or work and be fortunate or be born into luxury or suffer the wrath of poverty in a world that values consumption above all else. Step out the door and see how the landscape is molded around consumption. Stores on consumption of clothing, food, drinks and any empty physical item one could imagine. Modern man is also deeply confused, particularly in matters of career and love. Things which take a long time to figure out and can only have a few chances at getting right. The confusion of being dumped in a world that lets you choose your career out of every possible career in existence, yet provides no true or usefully comprehensive way of finding the right answer. Love too, is deeply shallow. As the modern men and women have no shared experience, and so fall back to empty and vapid choices like the physical appearance of a person on online dating platforms. Something which has never been a viable factor in the long-term success of relationships. Truth too, in the age of the internet one would think is a guarantee, yet has only proved to be nothing more than confusing noise. Anything searched online will only be confirmed and unconfirmed by one party or another, with groups on either side. Data shows what you want to see - confirmation bias - or the successful survivors of a result - survivorship bias - leaving nothing but noise. In the age of technology, an era presupposed to hold wonders and make our lives easier has only made things worse. Modern man has gotten fatter, lazier, more incompetent, lonelier and more anxious, no thanks to these technological devices. It is only through reflection and asking the question of how these things serve us and how they benefit us, can we move forward - which the modern man has yet to ask himself.

A Moment of Gratitude

A moment of gratitude, a time to reflect on the things which one has in the current moment so as not to be washed away in a torrent of gloom and loathing. I am grateful for the ones in life who I share this existence with. I am grateful for the incredible, mind-opening books I have read (granted not many), the wonderful experiences of some high-quality media too. I am grateful to be both full and able-bodied, currently in possibly the best health of my life this far. I am grateful for living in the current time, while, not perfect, beats the commonplace death, dirt and diseases of times past. I am grateful to have access to the internet and a library full of global information. I am grateful for my mind and wisdom and would not replace it with another - albeit perhaps a faster model. I am grateful for the beautiful places I have been and the places I will go. I am grateful to have a full belly and not have to do without. I am grateful for not the hardships one has faced but the ability to overcome them. Grateful to be in sound mental health and - for now - do not have to face such ill effects. I am grateful to not live in abject poverty and can afford the things I desire - albeit few and within reason. I am grateful to be born in a country which allows me to grow, explore and express one's potential. Glad to have access to a delicious variety of foods and drinks. Grateful for the sunshine and the touch of grass and the gentle breeze on a summer's day. I am grateful for the abilities, experience, knowledge and intellect which comprise me.

The Sugar Contract

Before ingesting any sugary food I must read the following contract beforehand: I will read this contract to myself and reflect on every single word and sentence. I will not rush through it but instead take the time to be fully aware of the action I am about to take. By ingesting this sugar, I am agreeing to the following terms - I am guaranteed to diminish my overall health and significantly increase my risks of a vast number of metabolic diseases including - but not limited to - heart disease, stroke, cancer, Alzeimers and dementia. I am increasing my insulin by severely spiking my blood sugar levels and tanking my energy and willpower for the rest of the day. I am also ruining any healthy streak I may be currently working on. I am directly depositing fat directly around my body, to which I will actively have to try to remove in the preceding days. I am contributing to nothing and ruining the teeth that I have and corrupting my gut biome, increasing the unhealthy bacteria that will only urge me to eat more sugar and increase my sugar cravings. I am directly putting money into the pockets of slimy conglomerates that don't care about my health and only wish to make money regardless of the consequences of others. I am setting a bad example for those around me - particularly the youth, which will be heavily influenced by my actions and may cause them to end up imitating me. I am conversely robbing my ability to show them how to do good and resist such temptation. I am also making the conscious decision to get a small, fleeting and momentary pleasure that lasts mere minutes and doesnt make me feel better afterwards, only disappointed in breaking one's streak and self-control and ultimately letting myself down in the process. After I have read all of this, I will say out loud the following terms: "I have read the contract and I have consciously decided I am going to eat sugar today".

Influence on the Child

The first and foremost of any authority to the child in terms of influence is that of the primary caregiver - most often the mother. A distant second, yet still vastly superior over others is the secondary caregiver - usually the father, then followed by the tertiaries - grandparents and/or family members at large. When there is a deficit and these members are lacking or non-existent, as in the case of death, neglect, abuse or absence, others in society step in to place their own values upon the child. Such as a society or a government. These rogue elements care not for the overall welfare of the child but would rather use them for their own nefarious needs. A government only wishes for a loyal peon - a soldier - one that would defend the political system for its own end to continue existing. Laying down the life of the child in order to keep the system continuing on. A society too, is no different in that the masses only want the child to parrot and mimic its own popularist ideologies. It is only in the caregivers, the primaries - often the parents. And only the good ones at that. Which do not wish to influence the child by way of mimicking its own worldview, nor to fight and defend to keep its political systems in power, no. But only to do that which is best for the child, what they want. What will please them and make them happy. Or atleast, the belief and directive of such a thing. Pure and untainted, doing what is best for the child and they alone, not one's own nefarious agenda.

The Child in the Window

Often as I gaze outside my window I see another place with a child in the window. No matter the time of day or the moments of time that pass, I look out and see him there. He is watching TV. Be it sitting on the floor or sitting on the sofa, but always watching the television for hours on end. He is young, looks no more than ten. With a large, protruded belly, an overweight boy. Addled with an excess of sugar and processed diseased food that is abundant in this century. Even with his weight, he still is like that of a young boy, boundless with energy. He rocks back and forth or waddles about as he stares at the screen, like something inside of him is screaming to get up and get out, but he doesn't know what to do, or to even realize it as he is just a young child. I see it all too well, the tell-tale signs of neglect. No one comes to him, no one takes him outside or teaches him of the world. Just a young child, so much potential and possibility all for it to be left rot in front of an empty, lifeless and loveless box. It pains me to see him as it reminds me of how I once was.

A World without Work

What kind of society will exist in a world without work? It seems with growing automation and mastery saved only for a select sliver of the populous, there will be no jobs for most. Or perhaps worse still, is that the majority would perform low-end meaningless labour. But regardless, how important is work? How much of a segment should it take up in our lives? It seems such a question has a wide response from empty hours to life-fulfilling and it is no surprise why. Take for example, how much of what a person becomes is largely environmental. If in one job - say a programmer - they spend all of their time alone, they work remotely. They have no office or see no-one. Take another job - a nurse - the turnover of new people they would experience would be huge. The patients they see, but also all the friends and family that would visit them. Co-workers too. It seems even in this example the environmental differences from two occupations are astounding. What about meaningful input? What of a tangible help to the community? What of their inverse? Contributing nothing and doing empty work? It seems that exactly because of the environmental weight jobs carry that it is of utmost significance. That so much can be tied into such a heavy choice and that - community, culture, atmosphere, peers, finance, meaning and more can all be derived from them. So then, what of a world without it all? What are we to do all day? It seems that it falls to the simplest conclusion first and possibly the most likely, that one would fall into a pit of consumption difficult to pull oneself out of. That existence would become nothing more than discussing and reviewing the latest books, movies and media. A large portion may even help create this content. Yet even now we struggle with the sheer amount of content available to us. It's hard to consider the ramifications if everyone became a creator and a consumer, past the point of a lot of empty noise. A more positive outlook is that perhaps in a world without work man has more freedom and time to adapt and grow. More time to develop oneself and bolster hobbies and talents. Improve one's body, read more, learn a language, a new martial art or instrument. Travel across the globe would open up immensely. New communities would be formed on improving ones-self and growing. Almost utopian like, yet I wonder, would money cease? What about talent, intelligence, fame, creative endeavours? I doubt it. For as long as humanity exists and our technology, so too will his inequality, and if money is not one way of hoarding power over the masses something else will simply take its place. For while science and technology may change the playing field the game is still ultimately the same. We are still human. We cannot escape from our illnesses and woes. Our biases and our corruption. We will find other ways to suffer without the sting of empty work.

A Moment of Appreciation for Science and Technology

Driving today through a long tunnel in a mountain. The journey took all of five minutes, yet made me appreciate what man has accomplished for a moment. We live in an era where we can fly. We can also move vast distances on land and sea too. We can learn infinite amounts of knowledge in the palm of our hands. Know that when we input a location into a device it will show us the path which will take us there and the amount of time it requires. Have a box that keeps food from expiring, while also being full most of the time with a varied plethora of goods from all over the world. We have inventions that keep us warm when cold and others that help us cool when we are hot. We have crafted artificial lights which we no longer need to sleep when the sun goes down. Other creations capture moments in time that will still remain long after both the moment and we have gone. We have built comfort in all our daily lives, from the clothing we wear, the places we sit and the areas we sleep in. We are capable of communicating with loved ones all across the world in an instant. And amongst all of it, we forget. We take it for granted and know no better. What an incredible creature man is! To create such wonders and forget just how remarkable this process all is!

The Most Powerful Question

Oftentimes, the most powerful question is generally the simplest - Why? This question, when drilled down can easily dismantle any long, complex thought processes. Why are we studying this degree? Why are we with this person? Why do we want this money? Why do we get up in the mornings? This deceptively simple, yet powerful question targets the very heart of matters and when used multiple times over, can help ease us of our confusions and burdens, holding up a mirror to ourselves and our miasma of thoughts. This potent question can often be so strong as to render us completely immobile, unwilling to let us take a step in any direction at all. Beware of this power, as all too often I have found its use debilitating, and the simplest choice is often never to do anything in its wake at all.

On Friendship

Concerning friendship, it seems modern man may find obtaining them more difficult than in previous generations. In the past, we shared locations. Experiences from one tribal group of peoples were similar. We lived in the same geographical location, hated the same opposing tribe and lived in lifestyles similar to each other. Now interests are splintered. What

I like, do, and occupies my time may be vastly different from the next person. Our lack of shared experiences also atomizes us to the point where it can be difficult for many to make friends. While we can somewhat remedy this by joining clubs, activities, and other shared experiences, some may find it difficult based on location or by joining a group that already has a tight social cohesion as an outsider. Then there is the nature of friendship at all. For example, is there a criteria to these friendships? Are they based on any strict principles such as honesty, integrity, reliability, intelligence, kindness, etc. or are they more related to the fact that the person is often in the same location, place and time as oneself. One must ask is this friendship based on principles that could last a lifetime, or are they simply superfluous and in the moment. An easy metric to tell this by is if conversation is deep, philosophical, beyond the surface, possibly even sometimes uncomfortable. A shallow friendship is often based solely on a similar theme, the environment, the workplace, a hobby, and never if ever deviates from that. In this instance that friendship will last for as long as they are in the same environment and no longer. One could argue there is nothing wrong with this kind of friendship, and keep juggling friends from one location to the next, picking them up and dropping them as you go. But on closer inspection it also holds a shallowness and an emptiness that could not be sustainable unless this person eventually found more stable and reliable friendships. How does one build a friendship then? Similar interests, compatible characteristics and repeated encounters, but also the ability to show vulnerability and appreciate their honesty when given. The rest takes time.

On a Second Language

Being a speaker of only one language, simply the one I was born and raised with being English - while also being the most globally used language, raises an interesting thought. Namely, that in being born with such an in-demand language, there has been no need for one to learn any other. However, English is only likely because of its growth across the UK and beyond in the early days of expansion - populating parts of Europe and finding its way across America with the settlers. Perhaps initially because of hard power - their militaristic might, but later their soft power. Because of the soft power of those countries - movies, TV, music, and tourism - it gained renown across other countries, particularly those in poorer countries, who had seen English speaking countries as an opportunity to move somewhere with better financial opportunity. What's interesting is that the language itself has no inherent value, it is simply popular based on its historical growth. It is just a tool of communication, no different from any other language. No different from Spanish, Chinese or Irish for example. There is nothing that inherently would keep a language sustained far into the future. Should another economic power come to rise we could all speak another language - Google-ese, perhaps! Learning another language makes for an interesting thought experiment - that the words we use are ultimately superfluous and come and go like the clothes we wear, across a vast span of time. And that while the sounds may change, the underlying principles still remain beneath them.

Changing Genders

Another change of the modern person which has risen and grown within the last decade or so is the radical growth and normalization of changing genders. Some believe that gender is an abstract concept and one changes gender as easily as the mood suits them. They may biologically be male, yet wish to be called "she/her" or biologically female called "he/him". Some even discard these typical pronouns and wish to be given the more general "they/them" or receive special pronouns which they create like "zim/zer". Some undergo surgery to change their gender into the other and change names while others do not. Currently this trend has spread predominantly around America and parts of Western Europe. This raises two key topics and concepts I wish to address, "the distinction of a mental illness", and "the effect of an atomized individual searching for community". On the first principal we have a sticky topic, how can we identify and separate an individual from a mental illness? Is this a person who is born in the wrong body yet has the opposite gendered brain or is this an individual who is so deeply unhappy with themselves that they wish to change it? How are we - the outsider - to tell the difference, as the effect of mutilating the body and introducing hormones in a differently-gendered body could have drastic consequences. There is currently too much emphasis in the way of placating, yet not enough of discovering do they genuinely need help. If it was another mental illness used as an example - say, social anxiety. How can we tell if a person is extremely introverted - a personal characteristic - or suffers from something that is controlling their life in a way that it wouldn't if they did not possess it - the mental illness being social anxiety which has hijacked their life. This important distinction between a genuine desire of a person with a brain different to the body they find themselves in and an illness that stems from disgust of the self is an important one to make, and one which we need to take better steps in understanding. This brings us to the second point "atomized individuals searching for a community". Humans seeking a community of peers is nothing new, nor different. This method is simply a fast-pass to find who supports radical ideas to find similar-minded people in the shortest space of time possible, that of "open-mindedness and tolerance". It is also no coincidence that many of these people are at an age where they struggle with the concept of an identity and are left as prey for those of ulterior motives, pushing their own ideologies upon those who struggle with themselves. Why would something as precious and fundamental as our bodies be the first piece to go, not tastes, clothes, preferences, habits, friends, environment, etc. Why can't these things shift but the gender of the individual remain the same? Because it is more. It is a radical way to set allegiances and draw ally and enemy lines, while the concept of gender takes a backseat to those who wish to join in a clubhouse of shared ideologies.

The Restlessness of Existence

For too long now life has felt restless. Like an insatiable crawling and itching to get away. Where no salve remains, and nothing can calm or ease this yearning to escape save for death. It is the uncomfortable feeling that nothing is worth obtaining, that nothing matters, and the process is an ultimately empty one of striving for things that don't matter. Pursuit of a career, for nothing save empty accomplishments and money that does not matter. All for fleeting and irrelevant experiences. Play games, watch shows, consume, all for an empty waste to pass the time. The boredom is relentless and nothing calms it or puts it to rest. Read books, learn, nothing works. Just an empty walk on a treadmill to distraction. Empty ways to pass the time as one marches pointlessly to the inevitable destination. I don't even remember anymore what I used to distract myself in the past, only that nothing works anymore. Only the unavoidable crawling under the skin, like a thousand relentless ants just waiting for the sweet release of death. Anything to stop the boredom of another day of pointlessness, another day of consumption, another day of empty distraction. It marches on.

Expectations, Reality & Fantasy

Expectations are the things which we expect will happen, for example we expect that when we go to college - regardless of the degree - we will get a good, well-paid, fulfilling and rewarding career where the act of going to college will be an interesting, fun and fascinating place to be. Reality is the thing that actually happens. Such as in the college example, college is actually a place where much of the degrees are fundamentally worthless, the degrees that have any worth are riddled with so much competition as there are only a limited number of jobs, the time you must invest in learning the prerequisite conditions to get, maintain and sustain this college/job career will consume a significant portion of one's life. College itself can also feel gruelling and deeply unsatisfying - with time-wasting courses and awful lecturers. That gap which I have used with the college example between what we believe will happen (our expectations) and what actually happens (the reality), I call fantasy. On observation and introspection, it seems that much of life is based in fantasy. The reason for this is simple. If all of life was based on reality most would kill themselves. Life would be too grim. It is the expectation for better - the fantasy that keeps us getting up in the morning. More examples: We expect that we will get a beautiful partner or many series of partners. They will please us in all the ways we desire, sexually, or they will serve our whims and we will never argue. This view of course is unrealistic. The reality is we will have long stretches of our lives having no-one at all. Some never even get anything. Then if someone does come along, they are not as pretty as we would like. They are a little old, or too fat, or something is off about their genetics. Or maybe they are pretty but they have mental issues, maybe they are too narcissistic, or obsessive, or paranoid. The relationship isn't as sex-crazed as one would have liked either, and instead over-time it becomes less and less frequent. They are not as compliant. They whine and argue. Fights happen more and more. They have male friends you think they like a bit "too much". They have parents who are unlikable. So many issues and examples of things we don't even consider, so many expectations which we will look up positively to make us desire something that we forget the harsh reality of things. A reality that when only considered, makes us not want to do anything at all. This is why we create fantasies. When the positive expectations meet the harsh realities. Jobs, college, career, friends, family, life. We create these fantasies to make it all bearable. We expect we will have a fulfilling career. We expect in our lives we will eventually make great amounts of money. We expect we will have many great friends we can talk to about anything. We expect we will have sexy, loving partners who will be completely compatible with us. We expect we will have compliant children who never stress nor bore us. We expect that life will be a pleasure. Full of excitement and enjoyment and not a stagnant drag. We expect so much and yet, reality guarantees none of it. What also happens is that we pander to others with these fantasies. We watch and create movies and TV shows that make these illusions seem real and possible. We tell each other that we can get the pretty girl, the great job, the large paycheck, all without anything guaranteeing it or backing it up, because reality - by itself - is not worth having. This is why many fall into escapism, when they cannot bear the reality of their lives. Books, drugs, movies, TV, video games, alcohol, gambling, all of it to escape - to take one's mind and thoughts away from the cold slap of reality. "Nothing is guaranteed. This is all a distraction. I dont have the girl / the job / the money. It's not what I expected. Nothing is what I expected and death awaits!". So what is the solution? Is it to lower our expectations so that they are closer in line with reality? To instead think, "I will get an average looking woman and we will only be partially compatible. We will fight sometimes and the sex will be occasional then rarer and rarer over time. Things will also stagnate and get boring over time too". Or for a job how about, "I will work really hard and spend a significant amount of time and effort improving my craft and knowledge to get a job. The market will be competitive and there are no guarantees so I will likely have hundreds of interviews and send out thousands of resumes until I might get a job and there is no guarantee I will like it. It may be stressful and boring". So you see the problem of setting expectations too low to reality is that it often puts people off doing anything at all. While the catch of having too high an expectation and getting nothing only to end up bitterly disappointed with reality, the alternative is setting expectations so low that we don't try at all. But then too, we are not fortune tellers. Our perception of reality is just that - an assumption. Unless we can tell the future we cannot know something completely. "Maybe we do get a great job that's fulfilling", we think to ourselves. "Maybe we do get the hot girl with nothing wrong with her". This constant back and forth between an unrealistic expectation and a low expectation that is impossible to predict keeps us tipping from one side of the seesaw to the other, in a world that cannot be completely predicted, with a faint hope that keeps us trudging forward.

What's the Most Dangerous Part of a Question

What's the most dangerous part of a question? It is believing you know the answer. Our world is full of chaos. Full of biases and fallacies, that when we peel back the things we know, on closer inspection we only think that we do. Once we have formed an opinion on a topic we shun conflicting viewpoints and only listen to echo chambers - confirmation bias. Or the things that we believe now, we forget and ignore the fact that we didn't always believe that way, and that in time, our beliefs will change again and again - hindsight bias. Or how we derive meaning from utterly random processes that clump together and weave a narrative that already corresponds to our confirmation bias - texas sharpshooter fallacy. Or how we don't even remember how we come to the assumptions and conclusions that we think we know and have simply been subtly primed, unconsciously nudged by others. Or how our mental blindspots have been filled in by being completely misremembered - confabulation. A question, once known, rarely if ever undergoes revision and the biggest fools are often the ones with the answers. All I know is I am an idiot!

The Three Stages of the Mind

Of the mind I would equate there to being three stages, the fundamental, the emotional and the rational, in that very same order which the mind had developed. The primary part, the brainstem and the core lower part of our brain is also our oldest, that which has been around for millions of years and is shared with the vast majority of animals on this planet. It comes with our essential components which allow us to perform actions

148

without any active thought: such as how to breathe, how to blink, walk, grasp, but also innate desires which we feel on a fundamental level to satiate us: the need to eat, sleep, procreate, socialize, defecate, urinate. These foundations are the building blocks which most of life share and the road which we drive on that leads to our decisions, to ultimately aid our desire to climb a social hierarchy, form groups and/or procreate in the process. The next is the emotional part of our brains, formed later and shared by less animals, but some still. Fear, anger, love, hate, disgust, jealousy, etc. all based on desires that steer and control our course of action. It is these emotions that control the direction we take in our lives. It is the reason why we do the things we do and the reason why we get out of bed in the mornings. If our innate desires (the fundamental) is the road which we drive on, the emotional part is the driver in the car that chooses the direction over the course of our lives. Our life being the car itself. The third and final part is the rational, the prefrontal cortex, responsible for executive function. The logical and rational part of ourselves. The part that takes over in the form of "willpower" yet depletes us over time. Metaphorically, one would liken this to the passenger in the car, the one who issues orders about what is the logically best choice. However ultimately, it is still the emotional part of the brain in control, as it is the moods that fundamentally dictate and control what decisions we take. Likened to how being in a fit of anger causes us to lose our stoic demeanor, or how depression causes us to lose our plans to exercise or take action. It is at certain times that the rational part of us can reach over and grab the steering wheel (willpower), but these are fleeting and ultimately the emotional driver is in control. The logical passenger tells us what we should do. The emotional driver controls what we actually do. On a series of twisting, turning roads that dictate what we as a species fundamentally want.

Strength vs Power

I want to discuss the differentiation between strength and power. Strength refers to physical ability. The condition of being able to exert their superior physical force on others. Children being the weakest, followed by (most) women, followed by (most) men of different types of physical ability and prowess based on weight, muscle, height, technical ability, etc. But power - power is an altogether different beast. I believe that power is the ability - whether implicitly or explicitly - which allows others to sacrifice their lives for it. This completely changes the dichotomy of strength and how it compares to power. Children are powerful. In that the parents will often innately sacrifice their lives in order to protect the child. Women too can be powerful. In that a husband will often sacrifice himself to keep the woman alive. Wars too have been fought, so that men could claim or protect women - sacrificing themselves in the process for a woman. Ironically, while men have the most physical strength, most men are completely powerless. Nobody would ever sacrifice themselves for them. So they form collectives. To institutions, governments and ideologies. It is in these collections conversely that the most power is held. A government is powerful in that it taxes its citizens and then uses this money to pay soldiers who will fight and die for that government, to keep that government alive so it can sustain itself. Ideologies too, can be powerful. An ideology is a way to maintain power, but so too is biology as we see with parents sacrificing for their children, so too is money (like the soldier) or fear (afraid of consequences that can happen if you don't risk sacrificing yourself). It's not that power guarantees sacrifice but that people are either at risk or willing to do so. On close inspection, one has to wonder: do you have power? Will you ever have power? And when you did have it, you certainly never realized it.

Rejecting the Modern World

In the current thirty-five years of life, the modern world has given me the following: A wasted life built upon by a mountain of consumption. Books, the internet, TV shows, movies, videogames - all of it has been enacted to separate the person's money and/or attention in place of valuable time, experiences and connection. A lie that hard work and education builds a desirable life, instead of a lifetime of regrets and misery. A modern world that has eroded community - at best a sanctuary of others who care for your well-being and replaced it with institutions that don't care about you, only what you provide, but have no shared experience or care for your life in the slightest. The modern world has cut the ties that bind us to others and now many feel deeply isolated, lonely and without any real connection. Any attempt to connect with another person is often messy, as people are complete strangers. There are no societal connections that ties us and many often find themselves stuck in topics of consumption, "What bands do you listen to, movies you watch, games you play, etc". All a desperate attempt to find some kind of commonality in an atomized world. Corporations peck at us like vultures so we end up with distended bellies, rotten teeth and lethargic energy levels. I hate it all. I despise it all. I don't want this, take it back. The modern world convinces the masses that money matters most of all and that it is worth the cost of throwing one's life away in the process. No value, no achievement, no creation, no community, no connection. Just a lifetime of consumption and loneliness at the cost of one's core.

Thoughts on an Ideal Community

An ideal community first and foremost should care about all of the people that are a part of this community. Before a community is built, it must set a standard that all members must adhere to and follow. Rules which every member will follow or be excommunicated, should they break these laws. These laws are built so that, should any member break them, they could fundamentally ruin or destabilize the community and the community is so fundamentally valuable to the people's way of life that the community comes first. Without core community values, families become individualized and splintered which then affect individuals. A community shares individual activities amongst its members in a shared environment to foster experiences amongst the tribe. Community farming, gardening, sports, dancing, can all be examples of this, where members all work together to accomplish goals and craft new experiences together. New rules and legislation to the community would be introduced carefully -

particularly by those who have been in the community the longest - to avoid dramatically impacting the community. This is especially important when it comes to disruptive science and technology - products that completely change society and how it is shaped with lightbulbs, cars, smartphones and social media being just some examples. Ideally laws that involve disruptive technology would not be integrated into the community, if at all, for several years, as it takes time before we see its negative effects. Such as social media creating fantasy, wasting time on parasocial relationships, taking time away from real relationships, etc. The community would understand the importance of good social ties, as well as mental and physical health so would contain a library, gym, conduct sports and engage in shared activities regularly. The community would not have a number large enough where people become strangers (around Dunbar's number of 150 or so) and the members would be regularly encouraged to spend time together from young and old, so that different generations could benefit from the thoughts and experiences of each other. There would be no mistrust and everyone would know everyone, starting from those core tenants the community was built upon.

Consequences of Community Absence

One of the most startling things to be noted in modern living is how fundamentally isolated it is. Let us contrast this with a thought experiment of how we humans lived previously. Man is a social animal, not a solitary one. For hundreds of thousands of years, if not millions, man and its species predecessors lived in groups and tribes. The world was a dangerous place, filled with opposing rivals, hungry predators and all sorts of other dangers. It made sense to collect together. The prefrontal cortex of the brain is believed to have grown and developed through these complex social connections that we sustained, similar to other social animals amongst other species. It also made sense to band together, as the work conducted by one can now be split up and lighten the burden. We don't need to sleep lightly and remain vigilant for enemies, as we now have others who will remain awake and protect us. We don't need to be an expert in everything as we now have information that can be shared amongst the collective. We don't have to watch our young - the weakest and most susceptible to dangers, as we now have others who can watch them while we hunt, farm, fish, etc. All of this shared living and existence would create a community. Contrast this to now. The modern human does not need to hunt or farm. Does not need the safety of a tribe to protect us from predators. Does not forge shared experiences with those in the same geographical vicinity, aside from those early days in education. Instead, people are highly atomized. Their culture, upbringing, religion, experiences, hobbies, interests, social connections are all so fundamentally different from one to the next, even among next door neighbours. Contrast this to the past where it would all be the same. Another issue is how modern humans talk about being shy, quiet or socially anxious. From an evolutionary perspective, man has lived for hundreds of thousands of years in groups, whom they would grow up together with. Anyone outside of that, would range from wariness to dangerous. It seems to make sense to be wary of strangers. And yet the modern world is full of them. Millions of them living around you, walking the streets. Is it any wonder man feels anxious, walking outside in a world of strangers, when he was built to live amongst his tribe? Then there is the matter of how people have become distrustful of others. In a tribe, we raised each other. Children of different ages and gender would play together, and adults would play with them too. The men and women would socialize together and the elders were seen as respectable and wise members, sought for counseling and guidance. Now, in this atomized world we are all strangers. Of course we don't want this man talking to children, or this one approaching this woman, we don't know them, we don't trust them. The atomization of the individual has led to the death of the community. Instead of children being looked after in a group of children amongst tribe members we often expect a single parent to shoulder the burden and bear the stress alone. Or put the child in a nursery, to be looked after by those who don't care for the child and are only there for a paycheck. Instead of elders being respected, we toss them away into a care home where they feel the weight of worthlessness and slowly lose their minds. Instead of teaching children in a loving environment, we toss them into a school. A place where dozens of strangers congregate that all have dramatically different upbringings. Some that have been prone to physical and mental abuse at home take this disease to the schoolyard and prey on others. Again the teacher is there for a paycheck and doesn't care for the individual needs of the students, only that they fill the criteria / pass the exams. People walk the streets and wonder, "Why am I so anxious?", or "Why am I so lonely?", oftentimes they will turn the blame inwards on themselves. Sometimes they will turn it outwards, to a bad childhood or negative parental experiences. But never will they stop and blame it on the environment. At how unnatural and fundamentally wrong it all is. At how community is gone and how we lost it when we left the caves/villages to the big cities for a paycheck, and in turn the price we paid in the end was far more than we could have expected. One has to wonder that a pattern should look something like this: individual, familial, communal, then on a broader scale: regional and possibly national at a governmental level. When we look at the self, we realize we have a certain level of autonomy in our behaviour, but at the same time strict and specific cardinal rules that must not be broken as they will critically harm or destroy the self. Similarly, this extends to the family. Cardinal rules in place that are put there so as not to destroy the family structure. This logic too extends to the communal levels and upward. Without community too, there is another issue, the disconnect between the individual and the government - the local and national rulings. Without community, the scope of the government is too large, and so it cannot possibly understand the plight of the individual and the critical issues that affect them. And so, there is a real disconnect. The connection between individual, family, community, and government isn't just bottom up - from the person upwards - but also top down. We see this often with how laws and legislation allows for advertisements to influence us, roads to take up our living spaces, addictions that have not been properly addressed, etc. Because again, the scope is far between man and government, and so laws are passed to benefit corporations and large industries over the individual. Communities too, have power. Imagine a place where everyone would fight with and alongside you, like you would for a sibling, parent or child, so it collectively has a power by the sum of its parts. This is not to say that community is the next political salve to capitalism, just to highlight how vital it is and how it is missing. For example, we could not all live life in self-sustaining communes, for how would we pay for roads or sustain a police force should there be killings or a court of law and judicial system. What about an army to prevent another country after noting we have all switched to communal living, coming and taking us all by force. It is explicitly by expecting the financial greed and ruthless competition of some, that others who care not for this kind of life can seek rest and recovery in a group that shares similar values and not that of the shallowness and competitiveness of the modern world. These communities would not be a basic form of geographical tribalism, not a sort of regression, but use and embrace knowledge and shared ideals to create a positive life with others. Set a rule, say, no physical violence. This communal rule then trickles down to the families then to the individual. Should a member break it, they are excommunicated. Such rules would be set by the elders to keep a healthy and long loving tribe, just as parents would with a family. This differs from traditional tribes where everyone sets their own individual rules and chaos reigns. This could be equated to a lawn left alone, weeds will grow and take over. But a carefully cultivated lawn can create something beautiful. A united, loving, caring, co-operation. One which is rarely seen in a modern capitalist society, where competition reigns and the money you make is more important than your character.

An Observation of Religion

While coming from a more agnostic perspective on religion, I wish to highlight some observations. First, religion is a concept that is supposed to be greater than the self, be it a vast incomprehensible power or presence that we can never hope to achieve alone, like that of an ant gaping at the presence of a man, we can but glimpse a toe and be easily crushed by such an expanse without even an awareness. It is something fundamentally beyond us. It grounds us, in that it reminds us of our frailty, our powerlessness, and the ever-looming presence of death that waits for us all. It holds wisdom in some of its speakers' lessons, despite being thousands of years old, and still holds useful excerpts to ways in which we can live - from Buddha to Christ - offering interesting perspectives which we can selectively incorporate into our lives. These characters, just as wise as we would expect from traditional philosophic greats, like Confucius or Seneca. It once bound us, from shared collective experiences together, and showed that we can work together from the individual to the collective in something greater than ourselves. We can see shapes of our own powerlessness in the natural world - from earthquakes and tsunamis, to the vast jungles, great canyons and wide mountain expanses. Both the natural world and religions share this sense of awe - that we are insignificant in the vastness of it all. Religion too, functions as a guide to live by, some incorporating powerful habits that have been grounded in scientific evidence as being healthy for us, like meditation, while others opt to use cleanliness and the emotion of disgust to steer our attitudes and desires as a consequence. A problem with religion, however, is that by creating and fostering a communal sense of cooperation and togetherness, it has also trapped itself in the rules and regulations of mainstream religion. Instead of seeing one particular religion like a chapter in the book of spirituality, it forces us into its boundaries. Instead of fostering one's individual connection with the spiritual - something that cannot really be done person to person, only experienced by oneself, like explaining colour to a blind man (known as qualia) - it is instead used to force and gatekeep based on ardently stringent tenants. While we still feel a sense of awe when we step inside a cathedral, the modern world robs a large sense of magic and wonder from it all. Look what man has accomplished - yes cathedrals - but look now at sky-high apartments, aeroplanes, cars, computers, and a whole host of new scientific discoveries. What religion can and still may do, is provide wisdom and guidance, inspire awe, shun generous acts that can destroy a community, inspire individual spirituality, while strengthening it as a group of people who yearn for a shared sense of commonality.

Do It for Them

Try a little experiment the next time you are undertaking some physical exercise. The next time you run or lift weights in your usual routine, exaggerate it. That gentle jog you are currently performing is now in the process of a long and grueling marathon. Think of a person in your mind - either living or dead, preferably living - and imagine now that they have passed. Imagine you are running with a picture of them emblazoned on your shirt, and a date of their timeline from birth to death, with the words R.I.P and "I do it for them". Think of how moments of your time together flashed before your eyes as you are jogging. Their smile. Their look. Their laughter. Think of that overwhelming feeling that will overtake you after a long and gruelling toll, when you cross the finishing line and your body crumples to the ground, overcome with emotion and exhaustion. You clutch the picture between your hands and look upon their face, tears begin to fall as the sadness washes over you and begin to weep. "I did it for you", you say to the empty photo as you kiss it gently and wail, even bringing all of the onlookers about you into tears, all too clear of the context. Imagine now, that you have all at once awoken from your daydream and are now still in the process of your daily exercise ritual. They have not gone, they are still here. Later you see them and reflect upon their death. You look into their eyes a little longer, smile a bit brighter and hold them a bit tighter. Reflect on the superfluous nature of existence and enjoy the present in their presence. Remember that death too will take them and not to take them for granted. Do it for them.

The Ephemeral Nature of Existence

Our being is nothing more than a tiny insignificant speck of time across human history, across all of history. Our life, no more relevant than that of a moth. All of our experiences, creations, and memories have nothing tangible to grasp onto, and rather, exist more like grains of sand which slip through our fingertips. On wants, on needs, on being, on our very nature - no more worth than the period at the end of one sentence in the tomb of a library full of tomes on the universe and all it contains within. Our grandiose accomplishments amount to an ant carrying a leaf back to its den or a worm that manages to wiggle out of the soil. Buildings to dust and bones to dust and words gone the instant one has said them. One snapshot of a person gone in the instance that they existed. We desperately clutch to anything yet the world is water and nothing we grasp at can be truly held between our fingertips - not beliefs, thoughts, friends, families, loves, fears, or self will remain in the blink of an eye we call "living".

The Madness of Cities

As I sit here and write this I am currently in a coffee shop in a big city, sitting on an uncomfortable stool and facing a large window, watching the crowds pass by. Perhaps this foreign man makes for quite the exhibit, both in how my appearance looks so starkly different to them, but also by the fact I am writing in a book with a pen, something rarely seen in the 21st century of phone-raised man. While I may appear like a zoo animal to those who look in, I believe the opposite has the same effect, that they pose quite the animal exhibit on the madness of cities and the crowds they inhabit. There is something distinctly unnatural about a city, in that of what it is and what it represents. Take man, who for thousands of years lived with some dozens of tribal members, intricately aware of each other and how they relate to us when growing up. Contrast that with a city of thousands of abject strangers, all of which with their own distinct lifestyles, traits and experiences. An intricate and wide array of complexities in one person, all of which passes before your eyes in but a millisecond. There's another. And another. Soon enough, you are bombarded with so many of these people that you must stop paying any attention to them at all, like one would with breathing or blinking. To do so you risk the danger of taking abject strangers for granted, but to not do so quickly becomes overwhelming to the senses. Another madness of cities is what they become, an empty mess of consumerism. Buy a coffee, buy an ice cream, buy some food, buy alcohol, buy clothes, buy gadgets, buy. It is as if cities simply exist to buy stuff. The sheer bombardment due to the constant noise, shops, and advertisement takes its toll, and one finds themselves buying more than they would when man is cool, calm, and at peace. The scurrying and shuffling of the masses feel at once like cattle, a man is easily led from one purchase to the next. Man is also far more rude in the big cities. Perhaps it's a combination of his anonymity, his worthlessness felt among the horde, this need to lash out to separate his face amongst the crowd and the empty and uncaring nature of the environment that all contributes to it. Presence in a city should not be taken lightly, as the nature, noise and overstimulation of the environment will make you tired, fat, unable to think clearly and fail to succeed in retaining focus. Therefore trips in the city should be treated like going out in the sun or swimming in the water. Keep your visits brief, and don't remain in it for too long or else it will cause you some harm in the end. Two more points I would like to mention involve movement and stillness. A city, when contrasted to a quieter life or of nature itself, has so much constant movement, while nature itself has so little, past the rustling of the leaves upon the trees and bushes, and the movement of some animals. Past this point, there is still a vast calm, tranquility and peace. The city life has noise, lights, movement from all the people and the vehicles, there is not a moment's respite. And now back to my original setting, about how I am sitting in an uncomfortable stool. That I believe is a core component of it all. The city is a representation of something purely capitalistic. Take your money, come and spend as quickly as possible and then take your junk and get out! There is nothing inherently as succinct in this as an uncomfortable chair in a fast food restaurant or a coffee shop. You made your purchase, we got your money, we don't want you to stay here for too long because we need the space so someone else can come in and we take their money, repeat the cycle. Hence, uncomfortable chairs. The city life itself seems built on similar principles. Keep moving, keep buying, don't stay in one place too long, don't get too comfortable, don't settle. Keep moving. Keep buying. To be still in a big city both looks and feels unusual. Look around, the majority of people are moving around, off to buy the next thing, off to the next store. Stillness here is rare. Most don't do it and when it scarcely happens it doesn't last long. There is a constant unspoken rule not to stay too long. Got to get up and move, got to keep buying. Mustn't dawdle, one needs to go and buy that ice cream.

A Critique of Social Media

While I have mentioned at separate occasions my intense dislike for social media, I will now try to attempt a more thorough critique of the subject matter, primarily to condense all of my issues with it here in one place. First I will bring to light the current players in the social media world, as I am sure it will no doubt shift and grow in the years to come. Currently the biggest social media marketplaces are: Facebook, Tiktok, Snapchat, YouTube, Instagram, Twitter, and Twitch. There are also big players in the eastern parts of the world, which I simply have not mentioned, but they are equally as diseased I assure you. It's also important to address that social media, if used in very small doses such as with loved ones as a way to keep the connection may be fine, but we will address this too later in my critique. My first critique of social media is how utterly pale of a comparison it is to real-life communication. Most of these platforms are little more than words of text on a screen, closely followed by an image, or a video. Let's start by understanding this, we went from a species that has grown and evolved communication and language, honed and calibrated over the course of thousands of years - learning body language, facial expression, vocal tonality, social context, shared experiences, all to be condensed to words on a screen. Left to be interpreted and misinterpreted. How can one be ironic, jovial, or sarcastic if the other party misunderstands the context of the other? While one may argue that words on a screen are prone to these problems, at least platforms that utilize images and videos are a step up from this, right? A picture is worth a thousand words, after all and video must be significantly more. This brings me to my second critique, how fake it all is. Both with images and videos, people tend to bias themselves, in that they tend towards showing only the best parts of themselves. Their best pictures, best lighting, best angles. Videos where we show ourselves looking good, interesting or knowledgable. This sometimes leads some to start altering their appearance with computer software, or talking about topics that they don't truly know about. Whether implicit or explicit, this creates a tendency to make us all too non-human, and sets a precedence for others to compete with us - particularly the youth - who may not understand that it is all a farce - all a game to appear better than others, to get more likes and validation (this will be my next point), all using angles and tools and snippets of a life that isn't what it actually presents itself to be. My third critique is the noxious dangers of external validation. With an internal sense of validation, or rather a stoic mindset, we base and calibrate our own sense of value and worth on ourselves - the things we can change. We can compare ourselves with all of our yesterdays and see how much we have learned and grown based on our past experiences and accomplishments. But external validation quickly becomes a very dangerous game. Our value comes from the likes and comments of others. Dangerous still, is the external validation that comes from abject throngs of internet strangers, all with their own hosts of illnesses, biases, and ideologies which they are all too willing to force down the throats of others they wish to follow along with their own current zeitgeist. Those who do not must endure anything from silence and rejection up to bullying, harassment, insults, slander, and forms of digital witch hunts - targets for a braying mob of hate. Thus, to be externally validated means one must conform. Conform to whatever works to get the validation or attention one seeks. Be it saying or doing particular things. But external validation too is chaotic. The winds of change blow so frequently that what worked yesterday does not work today. And so the externally validated person is always blown from one way to the next, while the internally validated remains steady and unchanged. A fourth critique is its unnaturalness. For something called "social" media, there is something inherently antisocial. In a face-to-face interaction you are seen, you are looked at, replied to, and acknowledged in some way, shape or form. In a social media setting, your comment may be posted and replied to after a period of time has passed or may never be seen at all. On a social media platform like YouTube for example, videos that have comments which range from the hundreds to the thousands have people making comments - but nobody replies to them or sees them - it is like the equivalent of having a loud conversation with yourself in an empty room. The comments section and the video may seem to give an illusion of sociality, but a lot of them are unsaid or unseen and have no value for it - sometimes people even pour their heart out or write reams of paragraphs but alas they waste their time. There is also the transaction of communication, and how that too has become impaired in social media. In a face-to-face encounter we have a discussion. We communicate. We say roughly an equal amount to each other. It is the transaction of sharing information and experience amongst each other. It might not be completely 50/50 in terms of our two-way communication, but close enough. In that, it is intrinsically tied to how we value one another. If I value you, I want to know what you have to say and I expect you would wish the same - which is why our communication balances out. If however, one party does not value the opinions of the other there becomes a skewering, a shift in the balance. Social media, by its own extension, shifts this balance. It is, by its own nature, unbalanced. A video creator could spend dozens of minutes to hours, talking about their struggles and hardships only to be met by a response by the viewer in a paragraph, sentence or even a word. The balance of communication is so uneven that it leaves both parties at a loss. The creator pours their heart out to no one in particular, and so strengthens their social bond with no-one. Meanwhile the consumer of the content may even feel attached to the person they have just watched, yet because of the communicative imbalance they are nothing more than a complete stranger to the other person - this is where we find the term parasocial relationship. Another issue is the question of comments of social media themselves, and how unnatural they are too. When something is typically said in person, it comes and goes. It is said then the rest of the conversation moves on naturally. If there is an issue in what is said it is swiftly clarified and addressed, and once again moved on. Not so with social media. Things said in person might travel like a breath of air but in the social media world they are more like photographs, to be reviewed, scrutinized and re-visited again and again, even years after it has been said. This warps a simple comment into something "other". A compliment meant once can be revisited again and again to boost one's ego. An insult can feel like a thousand knives. We leave much to the imagination, thinking "What did they mean by this?", rather than simply asking the moment it happens in person. Conversations are painfully stretched long and dragged out so that simple getting-to-know-you questions that could be done in moments are now pulled across the span of social media. See the text, wait minutes or days to reply and repeat. All of the emergency and importance of talking to the person next to you now put on the back-burner of immediacy, which brings me to my next critique. The fifth critique is its overwhelming loneliness. The utter irony of something that dares call itself "social" while all the while feeling completely isolating is akin to calling something that makes us hungrier "food", of which we have in spades - in the form of sugary, processed carbs and the like. There is something tantamount to psychologically isolating when one uses social media, in that you are alone. You are not spending time sitting and being in the presence of those you love, care and cherish being in your company - but rather - spending time in social isolation while viewing others who, at least give the impression, of leading more sociable lives than oneself. The psychological basis of wellbeing, at least in early childhood development, is the attention placed on the child over the course of many hours spent in shared proximity by the primary caregiver - often the mother, followed closely by the father. If not enough time and attention is put on the child, this can then develop into a host of issues and anxieties fostered on the core tenet of "I am not worthy enough because those who should be close to me are not". One cannot give these to a child while away, be it because of work, chores, other sociable ties or neglect. They can only be done face-to-face, in proximity, sharing experiences. A screen or a video of a loved one won't develop a deeper connection between the two - to harken back to an earlier point about ties with family members, it will only at best sustain them but not develop them. So if time and attention which are brought about through shared experiences and close proximity like that of a child and a parent, or any loved ones for that matter, what is the subtle implication of social media? It is that you are unlovable. It is that no one is willing to spend the two most valuable resources on you - their time and attention, and as such you must make do with a pathetic imitation known as "social" media where your message will be misinterpreted, you will see nothing but false images, you will be responded to when convenient like a table reservation not as a person, you will not be valued nor wanted, except for an ounce of dopamine that you will provide in their brains when you click a like button on their media and you will eventually pass from this world having made no impression to people, as no social ties have been strengthened nor developed with anyone. These are the dangers of social media: A poor communication tool, fakeness, external validation, unnaturalness, and loneliness. It is a slow and steady death of empty social ties while pretending to be in any way sociable. It is the modern version of cigarette smoking or drugs. It is a cancer and the less of it the better. I recommend it to no one, less they wish to keep their sanity.

On Philosophers

Philosophers have come in many forms over the years, from kings or riches, down to the lowliest ranks of poverty and slavery. But what binds them? Why them and not all of us? One of the reasons I believe is needed to make a philosopher is simply free time. A man preoccupied with busy work has no space to mull over other things. Those who are kept busy, be it to keep a roof over his head and food in his belly, or distracted by his passions or simply running about performing empty busy work, have no time for philosophical thoughts. But okay, time we have gathered as much, but many people have time - some too much time in fact, yet have no interest in these thoughts. Which brings me to my next reason, what is constituting their thoughts? Some try desperately to have no thoughts at all, learning that to be in their own head is a source of misery and so delve into the world of distractions - drink, drugs, consumption - all to keep the mind busy from focusing on itself. While others, keep the sight of their thoughts, the "mind's eye", if you will - focused on other endeavours. Some are on their social-ties, family members, friends, and of those they wish to know and ascend their ranks, the socialites of the world. Others focus their thoughts on calculable science and mathematics of the world, the scientists. Others still, on art, music, or poetry. But a key point to press on is that philosophy itself is just a segment. All of these people, these philosophers did not live all of their lives with philosophy at the forefront. They still ate their meals, took to the toilet, romanced a partner, played with their children, laughed with their friends, enjoyed the sights, conversed with neighbours, and walked their dogs. They were still people. Philosophy was what was done in the cracks of their lives in between living. Aurelius may have philosophized but he was still a military leader, no doubt involved in the stratagems of his day. Seneca would write but would also have to deal with his finances for his accounts and properties. Plato was a thinker but he also laughed and played with his children, no doubt. It is easy almost to imagine philosophers as a different creature, immovable, unshakable, stoic and pure calm regardless of the situation, like those stone and marble busts of those ancient early Greek philosophers, but at the core, they were just people - leading regular lives, and philosophy was the spice sprinkled on top of an otherwise observant existence.

Multiple Selves

Something which bears greater reflection, that all too many fail to acknowledge is how there is more than one self, and how these aspects of us influence our behaviours when navigating the world. And that, within these selves, will you find no two alike. The current self now which is both writing this and reading it could be considered the "thoughtful" self. One of calmer, analytical disposition. This is the self that appears on reflection, or the self that writes philosophy, or is thoughtful of his current day. But he himself is frivolous, he comes and goes in a moment's notice, like all the other selves. Should someone waltz up to him now, scream in his face and punch him, he would be replaced by an all too different self - one of anger. This version of ourselves is all too like a raging ape, intent on quelling what caused him to make his appearance. The future prospects and long term implications be damned for a one such as he. But what of lust, and his short-sighted pleasures, the instant gratification and action that can make us look like fools. Many of us set up plans and routines when we are in a nobler disposition, yet utterly fail when our tired or hungered self comes to visit. It is why we never meet the angered or sullen philosopher, only the philosopher, as any other self simply isn't interested in such a work, as to try something when in another state of mind dulls the work. Can one be a thoughtful boxer? After the bout has finished and one wishes to reflect on the rights and wrongs of the fight, certainly, but in the heat of the battle? Should the wrong self appear it would result in tragedy. What about a fearful fisherman or a lustful firefighter? They result in a misalignment and simply don't work. But enough on the subject of work, how can we make better preparation when it comes to the self? By being aware that there is more than one self. That by understanding when we make plans about how to eat healthy we are making them when we are currently in a state of satisfaction, but we must also make plans for what to do when the hungered self comes to call. For example, having something easy to make and accessible, fruits perhaps. Or if the lazy self makes an appearance, having pre-cooked meals already at hand in the refrigerator. Or even making the decision to avoid the "hungry self" at all, such as eating before becoming too hungry - or rather - not giving the hungry self any power, like going shopping when in this disposition. All too often, many don't realize we have these other selves, yet companies, sales, and marketing know this all too well and try to push us to spend impulsively, forgoing the "let me think about it" mentality, with one of a more reckless impulse, "Buy now, you can't miss this opportunity! Limited sale! Last in stock, etc.". Many are surprised by the stoic nature of a person, only to be greeted with one of a completely different disposition when angered. What did you expect, are they not now different men? And so too does the philosopher bury his head into his hands with shame when he realizes the consequences to their heated actions. Or the lover who has slipped out of the relationship for a side of secret passion. Do not act too quickly in the moment, if what you wanted was the calm and thoughtful self, for they have gone, replaced with another, who may look the same yet have entirely different plans to the deeds that are about to be carried out.

Dwelling on my Own Incompetencies

An illogical fool who says one thing in a moment, yet completely changes one's stance over time in the next. Held together with a brain of thoughts likened to a bucket filled with muddied water and riddled with holes. What use is a leaky bucket? What worth for a brain that holds together thoughts, knowledge, facts, yet is altogether ruined by its own perceptions and degrades over time. What a fool, to narrate one's life in an elaborate tapestry from birth to death in a desperate need to try to cobble together some sort of make-shift worth and purpose beyond something that is altogether insignificant in the grand scale of things. Why do you even wake and get out of bed? For an empty drudgery of one's day until the faithful end? Fool, worth no less and no more than all the others, locked away in a high-tower of one's own delusions and anxieties. What worth are all your theories? Have they all been rigorously applied? Empty assumptions and nothing more. And why do you waste so much of your days in worthless activities so? Empty consumption and the like. Especially when you know that they bring you nothing? It is as if you are nothing more than a beast in the guise of a man, living life on nothing past your base impulses and proclivities. The trickery of all these thoughts is that you are just trying to fool yourself into believing that you are something more when you are nothing but a lowly animal, like all the others about you - utterly common - high tower or not, and your thoughts and writings are as useful as used toilet paper.

Thoughts on Land Ownership

Something that concerns a finite resource will often result in tragedy. This is no different with the topic of land ownership. Land, in its essence, is limited. But also when concerning the types of land, being that the location of the land, the weather within that specific region and its access to a nearby supply of water, all result in different qualities - from a rich and fertile crescent, to barren and dead, where nothing can grow. Let us not forget that there was a time when we would fight to obtain better land. Not riches, nor religion. Not ideologies, nor women, but the land itself. The basis and bastion from which a successful culture or civilization could grow. In the modern era we are left with a dilemma. As income inequality grows, less people have more money, while more people have less. This then results in the wealthy buying up vast quantities of land, not just in one's own country, but in optimal places all over the world. This results in dramatically higher property prices and many empty properties, with these wealthy elites content to wait for a buyer to come along while the land is wasted in the process. It is not just that land is snapped up quickly by the elites, but also the types of land too. As mentioned prior, different locations have different qualities based on soil fertility, but also based on scenic views, or locations near busy cities. And so, properties in cities, towns, beaches, beautiful locals, are snapped up and it is left to the common man to make do with the scraps in the process. Often we now have the issue of the land itself, as in the ground - the fertile soil of the Earth. Where people must make do with instead of building lengthways and widthways, we must build upwards. Higher and higher we climb to the clouds, in vast sprawling apartment complexes. Where we are no longer man amongst the soil, free as a king to do as he wishes with his little piece of land to craft and grow as he likes. But is now suspended in a box in the air, cut off from the rest of the world and all of his interactions with it. Robbed too, of the joys of gardening, and of feeling the grass between one's feet.

Gardening

Something about gardening makes the concept an altogether satisfying one. Perhaps it's the careful crafting and cultivation, perhaps its the steady development of ones growing crop which ultimately results in a fine harvest or a beautiful landscape, perhaps it's simply being amongst nature, and seeing some slight integration with the world around us as the bees pollinate the flowers or the earthworms enrich the soil. Whatever the reason, there is a gentle satisfaction that comes with gardening. It is a wonderful skill to teach the youth. It can be done in a community to help bolster our social ties in shared proximity. It can be used as a useful pastime for the elderly - not just for the healthy, fresh crops of fruits and vegetables we can grow, but also for the mild exercise accomplished in the process. It teaches all of us to be patient. That in the natural world, growth and reward takes time. That patience - one of the greatest of virtues - can be subtly reinforced in such a way. That we can eat, secure in the knowledge that we have avoided any harmful chemicals. That we have created something with our own two hands. Few are those who sing the praise of gardening, yet it is a golden standard and skill which all should live by and undertake.

Distractions

We fight in an ever-constant war against distraction. All too often our families, friends, children, colleagues, and even complete strangers take up time in our lives, drain the willpower we have to achieve our goals and take up space inside our minds, claiming land over ideas that may now never grow. Now more than ever, big businesses and companies make it their mission to distract you as much as possible. Keep your eyes on the screen, keep watching, click this ad, your data is valuable to us and all too often we submit to them. How often have you had goals and ideas one moment and then after a few emails, a few videos on a video platform, completely lost such desires? We must make peace with the fact that we will be distracted – at times unavoidably so – but it's important to remember to carve out times specifically and only for ourselves, and no other – not even our loved ones – in order to push ourselves forwards with our goals and developments and to pay particular heed to the dangers of distractions from the corporate world and the digital one, remembering at times we must shake off the static noise and give breathing room for ourselves and our aspirations.

One thing to be certain of is how desperately man claws and thrashes about distracting himself. That the fundamental consequence of thinking too deeply on his state of things can bring about a misery so profound he must silence his thoughts in order to sleep tonight and rise out of bed in the morning. That the body we so carefully sculpt and craft today, will grow frail and broken with time or injury, then bones, then to dust and cannot be taken with us after. That our partners will grow old, lose their minds, and their bodies and be gone from us. That our children will not believe the same things we do, reject things we say, see us less as time goes by and only think of us in brief footnotes. That the wealth, knowledge, and possessions we obtain slip through our fingers over time. Things break. Money is spent, or worse - never spent. And we forget, so many things. That the friends we obtain are often brief chapters in the tome of our lives, often bound only by location and experiences. That anything and everything we do is compounded by a state of present numbness - to be only in the present so as not to dwell upon an ounce of one's life. Where am I going? What am I doing? What is the point of this job? This relationship? To what end? So we try desperately to swim upwards from the depths of these thoughts to the shallow surface waters of distraction. To live for today, to hell with these thoughts. Let what come may come. Drown them out.

Declining Birth Rates

It seems that our species may be extinguished one day, if we are not careful, not with a bang but with a whimper. More nations now are having less and less children so that these nations are slowly being bred out of existence. This is a particularly looming disaster for first world countries, who are leading the charge in this crisis. But why is this happening? One at the forefront I must imagine, stems from money. We have a crisis of money in this world. Not just the inane pursuit of it to our demise, but in how we rush and strive desperately for things that seemed so much easier to attain in our forefathers generations - property being a large one. But not only properties. Properties, lands, clothing, gadgets, fine foods, travel, subscriptions and utilities. Our wants have grown, but our needs - like that of human connection - remains. We want a loving partner, children, a family and a shared life together, yet we waste time on empty titles and pursuing wealth that does not matter. And so too is there a desperate clutching for a job. Any job. A better job. A raise. This pursuit for a career stops and slows many from ever finding a relationship at all. Then there is the case against technology. It is like the social band aid that keeps us from trying. Why step outside the front door, dress ourselves up and make awkward, uncomfortable small talk with strangers who we likely will never see again, when we can just stay within the safety and confines of our homes, of our rooms. When the alternative is to stay at home, in our comfort bubbles, indulging in small, low-level entertainment that passes the day in a mild state of numbness. To touch upon another reason just mentioned, safety. It seems there are growing numbers of those with anxiety and perhaps this, too, is a consequence of less social connection and overindulgence with technology. That we shelter ourselves in our boxes, safe and comfortable in the things we only wish to hear and enjoy. All the while consuming catastrophic news articles purely designed to get our attention. The world is declining, others are out to get us, this country will invade soon. All of it desperately clutching for our attention while pushing us further into the depths of anxiety and individual, atomized separation. A final point to these declining birth rates is population disintegration. With the dual-pronged attack of increased competition in the job market and cheaper and simpler airline travel, it's easier now than it's ever been before to leave our familial homes in pursuit of a better income. This leaves families separated and splintered. While the child has moved abroad, the parents are left at home. This constant moving of people also makes it difficult for community to develop and spread its roots, allowing people to socialize and meet in authentic environments, where people already carry some renown about themselves - instead of the plague of social media where a person can be nefarious and manipulative, and we would know of no better, and as a result their reputation cannot be harmed. So I ask, with all the time we invest pursuing money, distracting ourselves with technology, riddling ourselves with anxiety and atomizing ourselves from our cultures and communities, is there any wonder the global population keeps declining?

Governments

First to clarify, governments are - for these intents and purposes in time - necessary. They fund the essential components of a country to stop its collapse. They fund the fire service to prevent our houses from burning down. The hospitals, should we sustain serious injury but cannot afford it. They provide the military, which prevents an invading army from taking over and completely overwhelming our nation's rules and regulations, at best. They fund a police force to enact and enforce justice when needed. Yet on the other hand, just as easily as an army or police force can protect and provide defence, so too do they send young troops off to die needless deaths and turn the police force into mindless pawns, enforcing only what the corrupt higher-ups deem them to. A government does all it needs to in order to keep itself alive. Be it building up its own power or destroying others that it sees as a challenge to this power. It carves up territories across the land and demands it controls all within its borders and all must answer to it or face its wrath. No man is safe to try and build himself up from nothing, without things being done in the specific way that the government deems. Wish to start a business? Open up a stall on the street? Play about with that land you own? Leave the country? Try to make a sale with another person, one-to-one? Not without the governments say so. While it may be argued that some rules are needed to prevent a collapse of the society - perhaps if everyone could open a market stall they would crop up everywhere and cause obstruction - others are just nonsense. One cardinal mistake was allowing the carving up of land - piecemeal by piecemeal. Now for the price of a cheque, one man could own vast acreages while thousands are boxed in together with nothing to their name. Others still from other countries can own property in completely different countries. To think, vast swathes of one's homeland is owned by a wealth that has never even set foot upon the soil! It too, this government, forces education upon us. Knowledge is a beautiful thing, of this there is no doubt. But some governments make it mandatory, to force the same track of schooling upon everyone, with no guarantee of a job for the vast majority of them, the idiocy! But the worst part of a government is its inherent corruption. Human beings, ultimately care only for a sliver of people - themselves and their own personal loved ones, friends and family. In its very nature they give personal preferences, both nepotism and solipsism, the benefits of jobs, gifts, and offers to friends and family members. Governments in their nature too, are hierarchical. There is either one at the top or many. Over time, even in a "good" government, wicked agents will eventually bubble to the top and in such a powerful system with no external agent to answer to, they will be impossible to remove, without complete governmental collapse. It is in wicked governments that do the following: restrict those from moving in and around or out of the country, prevent free education - such as libraries while forcing education such as mandatory schooling, inhibit creatives and entrepreneurial endeavours, enforce them into servitude to go and die so that their own power grows. And most blatantly, silences and/or kills those that speak out negatively about the government. The government is not a God. It is not a separate entity that rules over all of a nation's meager populous, no, but it is the vessel of the people. It must grow, from individual, to familial, to communal, to governmental (regional and/or national). Without such, there is a gaping void which disconnects the person from the government. The government at best is a nation's sum of its parts that accomplishes that which we cannot possibly do alone, with our own small-minded and selfish wants and needs. At worst, it is the abusive parent that beats or kills us whenever we cause slight to its overbearing demands.

Call of the Void

The void is the destructive part of ourselves that yearns to return to what it once was - the nothingness. The emptiness. To lay waste to all of our endeavours - the attempt to socialize, to eat right, to learn, to mold our bodies with hard work and determination. It wishes to undo it all and revert us back to our former selves - the one we have faced before birth and will face again after death. The void calls us to take it all away. You don't need friends or family. Eat all the unhealthy slop you desire and allow one's body to turn into a jellied mush. Some days the call is silent and unheard from. Other days the void is all one can hear. What worth is there to tell oneself to forget it? To distract oneself with noise, it doesn't work. The call is always there. A reminder that the movie will end, the story will close. And that will be the end of this endless drone. This series of endless distractions until we reach the finality of death. We see only the subtlest of hints of death around us. In the news stories, in the animals we eat daily, in the close loved ones that pass. But the news deaths are only a detached statistic. The animals have their feathers plucked and heads removed, we see no animal. And the close loved ones are a brief slap of sadness before we lie still, in pure silence, in the depth of our thoughts and realize that the call of the void is only for us.

The Fragile Alliance of Long-Term Partnerships

By long-term partnership, I am specifically referring to those in a long-term relationship, such as a marriage or romantic relation that has lasted for many years. Much of this too applies to short-term relationships, but each are wrought with their own unique issues. The modern long-term relationship can be considered like that of a fragile alliance, as all the terms and conditions are in a more constant state of flux than they were many years prior. Take religion for instance. Prior to the modern age, religion stood at the apex of marriage. It stood precedence that over the eyes of God himself, the marriage was held sacred and sacrosanct. That his present and all powerful gaze would be ever watchful. But not only this, but so too would our families, friends, neighbours, and others - importantly - not strangers. These combined with our own beliefs and fears of the consequences of breaking such immutable laws like one of marriage. And now? What religion? For something that may have held prominence in the past has crumbled into something more individual and atomized. God for many either does not exist at all, or is a cherry-picked package of beliefs and superstition. Marriage as a consequence, holds little sway in a being that may either be indifferent to one's marriage vows or non-existent in the process. Then there is another matter, one which has shifted from the past thanks to disruptive technology (again, this meaning technology that has come about which has fundamentally changed the way we live our lives, think fridge, television, lightbulb, car, internet, etc. In this regard I am referring to social media and the harm that can be done to relationships by it. Think in the past if one wanted to develop an intimate relationship with another person. They would have to slip away from their partner and spend time searching for a new interest. More time then romanticizing this new interest, then more on being sexual with them and continuing the relationship beyond that to maintain it. Much time would be required and then physical absence would be noticed - if not by their partner they may be spotted with another person by a friend / family member or neighbour and be found out. Not now. Much contact by other sexual suitors can be found through social media, where relationship building, flirting, sexualizing, can all be built up right before that once inevitable meetup. The partner is none the wiser, and is unable to prevent any would-be escalation since they are unaware of it. What about checking a partner's phone regularly to be certain? This would be a madness, only to lead to paranoia and relationship ruin. The best course in this regard is for both parties to refrain from social media, of which certain people would struggle to do so, like those with high external validation. Then there are aspects that are not new in the fragile alliance of long-term partnerships. Issues that have been around since the dawn of time, like that of stagnation and decay. For one thing, humans are highly novelty-seeking creatures. We yearn for new things. New environments, information, enjoyment, experiences and - namely - relationships. The attention of new experiences and conversations can be alluring to some. Take these age-old issues and combine them with the modern shift of disruptive technology, making finding new potential partners easier and the ever-watchful presence of God fading away, is there any wonder that modern relationships face a greater threat than ever before? And then decay. We are aging creatures. We get old and lose our looks. Our energy levels are not the same as it was in our youth. We do things less, we try things less. Our energy levels lower and we get tired easier. We get set in our ways and become boring (lack of novelty), to which our partners may yearn for elsewhere. The ironic piece however - should you choose to leave a relationship and join a new one - is that all of these issues are still ever-present. The temptation for new, the stagnation, the decay. And that fresh juice of novelty that we are ever searching for to chew is like that of gum, where its flavour will eventually fade and we must decide: Do we continue chewing on a stale piece, keep replacing the piece with a fresh one forever until death or spit it out and convince ourselves that chewing is a bad habit anyway. A final caveat to something relevant in the past but now no longer is that of danger. We needed each other in the past deeply more than we do now. Without one we may lose our financial provider, or the carer of our children. We would lose protection against those who could rape, murder, and destroy everything we own. Thankfully we don't need to worry about our property or physical safety anywhere near as much as we used to, but the inevitable consequence of this is that we don't need each other quite as much.

After Utilitarianism comes Shallowness

For many years, individual humans have continued to exist because their utility kept them alive. It was all thanks to their own two hands that they could hunt and kill the animals, forage through the bushes for nuts and berries, reap the fields for a bountiful harvest, work gainful employment to earn the tokens needed to put food in their bellies and a roofs over their heads. But over time things changed. Large sweeping corporations came in and displaced many local workers. Training and education drove upwards, making the barrier to enter the workforce higher and harder. Governments stepped in to provide wages for the jobless. And now a man can live in an era that was unprecedented for all of his entire being - he could live without having to work for his living. No longer did he require a skill or a craft to tangibly continue his existence. Now he can live without having to do anything at all. This has created a shift in human values. A man is no longer deemed by what he can contribute to the group, as it can be found from elsewhere - governments and corporations. And so we have placed greater emphasis on shallow features in its stead. What a significance to the group a hunter would be. Or a baker, tailor, mechanic, singer, or any infinitude of professions. But now no longer. One is replaceable. And so greater emphasis is placed on how one looks in this superficial world. How is he with his community? Does he have a good reputation? Is he honest or deceitful? Is he helpful, does he volunteer? Well, what community? Such a thing is long dead. So next, one emphasises the gym. His abs, jawline, muscles. All superfluous and empty, containing only trace amounts of something those muscles could have been used in during our evolutionary past. What of the woman, is she wise, intelligent, kind, caring? The modern world cares not - just dance,

dance and look pretty. Once we have deprived ourselves of a need to exist, shallowness ultimately takes its place and our "usefulness" lies in how pretty we are.

The Positive & Negative Reactions of Childhood

It stands to reason that an individual's course of life - in their interactions with others - can largely be attributed to the set of events during their childhood and adolescent phases, primarily that of early childhood. It is during this time when we are at our youngest, while simultaneously at our weakest and most helpless, that we develop the core and critical lifelong skills of how we integrate and interact with other human beings. It is from our primary caregivers - often mother and father - that we are given a set of social tools that we take with us for the rest of our lives. Should our parents be loving, patient, considerate, playful, curious, and intelligent, we find ourselves bolstered by them. With these tools passed onto us, we expand out of this bubble of safety and dare to venture outside into a dangerous, unforgiving and unloving world, knowing none the wiser. Armed with the love of our parents, we can risk to be a little more boisterous, a little more gregarious, are more willing to take more risks and show a little bit of our sillier sides. During adolescence, we come across as a little more likeable, more confident and more sure of ourselves. Contrast this with the other. Core, primary caretakers who are missing, neglectful or abusive. Our safety bubble has been compromised. The time we are supposed to learn and grow during our vulnerable infancy has now been wrought with chaos and insecurity from parents that are uncaring, spiteful, stupid and inconsiderate. We grow unsure of ourselves and - the key critical point - deeply untrustful of the world around us. We grow anxious and ashamed, struggling to meet the gaze of others or looking at interactions as a form of confrontation. School during the time of adolescence becomes a prison, surrounded by threatening others. We then grow into adults, wary and unwilling to reach out and trust anyone, all of whom harboring unknown and ulterior motives. The world becomes a grueling place around us and we are indelibly marked during a critical point in time, where we had no control of our own existence.

On Logic Against Emotions

One thing on this matter is clear, that is logic can never win in a battle against emotion. What worth is it to look at a long list of metabolic syndromes caused by an unhealthy diet of drink, sugar, and fatty excess? One could remind oneself how our lives are shortened, how we give ourselves unwanted addictions that lodge themselves in the mind and gut, at how we make ourselves lethargic and sleepy. A volley of studies, graphs, and charts all made to please and pander to that part of ourselves that is pleased by such a thing. And yet, most of it falls upon deaf ears. We please ourselves with facts but ignore the giant beast who holds all of our power - our emotions. Not singularly either, mind you, but a variety of different beasts that must be prepared for and tackled separately. Those of anger, sadness, depression, anxiety, happiness, boredom. We spend our time trying to logically justify the things we do yet do not readily prepare ourselves for the weight of our emotions. How does a sugar addict console oneself with facts of cancer and stroke when they swim in the depths of sadness? Or how a smoker, when battling with anxiety, must arm themselves with lung damage trivia? No. Only by tackling the emotions themselves, by shifting to a more manageable one, or lessening the damage of the one we find ourselves stuck in can we ever hope to win in a battle against ourselves. Stress must become de-stressed. Boredom must be tolerated. Anger must be calmed. Sadness must be settled. In my own personal experience, I have had first-hand failure when it comes to battling emotion against logic, particularly when it comes to sugary food. The sugar contract I had written previously failed. I made a sugar journal, where dates, descriptions, and emotions felt at the time could be written down so that maybe I could see a pattern. Perhaps I could determine a logical system, noting the causes, and devise a particular scheme that would work. On and one the logic would spin, only to fail instantly when stressed, tired, or depressed. It simply cannot work. Logic takes time. It is crafted carefully in a battle of back and forth arguments and explanations. But emotion is instantaneous. It acts the moment it is felt. For this reason, logic cannot win when it comes to short-term actions. Only emotion can beat emotion. Particularly an emotion that can be "faked" in the early stages, and also turned on and off at will. Something that can correspond directly to our desires and wants. One powerful emotion in this regard is disgust.

A Piece of Me

This book is a piece of me, in that it is my thoughts. Granted, thoughts can and may change over time based on new experiences and knowledge altering our perspective, but still a piece - one which I hold in dear value. Strange then, when we consider how little of our thoughts are heard or shared with others - only in segments of books, texts, and the internet. Often others only hear our words, see our habits, or our actions, thoughts making but a small piece of it all. Most, even those closest to us will only ever see our actions, and only some of our thoughts which have been filtered out into our words. Our thoughts being the most guarded, are often those most rarest to be shown.

Short Notes

Some shorter thoughts listed below:

- The man who wants nothing will get exactly what he wanted.
- What separates men who create shit from men who create diamonds? The men with diamonds have greater mounds of shit to sift through!
- How much control or will do we have over our own lives and how much of it was preordained by our parents, grandparents, great grandparents, society, culture at large and how much of it will continue to be influenced during our own existence? When I consider the aspects of a free will, I often find it to be a losing battle. At the very least, an exhausting thought.

- I see countless advertising posters of sexually provocative women posing over the latest worthless plaything of the day. I am not immune to my own desires, either. I want to eat when I am hungry, it's all I can think of. I want sleep! I want sex! I often think that man has not shared a common ancestry with chimps, rather we are just chimps in suits.

- Can a man change who he is only after years of hard work or in the instance he decided it? And the body's simply taking time to catch up.

- Do we have purpose? Does life have a purpose? Is there a reason man yearns for one or is it indoctrination, like the things we consume and the toys we buy? Do others have a purpose? What purpose is there for the factory-farmed chicken? The unlived life of a stillborn? The empty minds of masses? Do we have purpose?

- Self-doubt comes to nest over the period of inaction and tries to bury itself firmly amongst the words and criticisms of others who tell you it cannot be done. It can only be shooed away by action. A journey comes about by its first single step. A book written comes about from its first chronicled word. A lifelong friend or partner comes about from the first, tentative "Hello".

- A past you is not a future you. A hungry you is not a content you. An angry you is not a sad you. You cannot hold it against yourself. We can only accept the fact that we embody change, that change is contradictory at times, and we are all just a bunch of living contradictions.

- People would rather give pride of place to a lump of shit from a somebody than a diamond from a nobody.

- To offer something to the masses without any fame about you is like that of running a horse race without a horse.

- Do not regret. Regrets are like scars upon the mind, sensitive to the touch. They cannot be changed, only avoided. They are in the past and will remain upon one's mind until the end of our days. Only can we make better choices today that influence our tomorrows, hoping that their results provide a soothing balm to the yesterdays that stung us so.

- Better to dig a ditch for your community than to give your soul to the world.

- Three things one should pursue greedily: sunshine, knowledge and laughter.

- You know that awful feeling when you walk past a room and hear people talking badly of you? Now you can get it constantly thanks to social media. Why would anyone choose this?

- You as a living being are entitled to only one thing: Death.

End

Much of our lives are reserved for a special kind of person, those who make it to the end. Those who watch a video to the end, are the ones who read a book to the end (except for those who skip to the end, I see you), and those who are there at the end of our lives. These people are truly wonderful, and the ones who we dedicate much of our resources and energy to. In this regard, I want to say thank you for making this journey with me and making it here until the very end. Not many choose to do so, in all endeavours, but in this case you did. Thank you for humouring me and listening to these fragmented thoughts.

This is the first and only book I have ever written. This book was made somewhere during 2019 and was continued on and off until mid 2023. It was always a long-term goal of mine to make a book, and so finally I started putting pen to paper, just a couple sentences here and there – a couple of pages on other days. It was very cathartic for me – and satisfying for me to have a creation, a project that was all my own. I hope you gleamed something of use from this book, and if you found this book in anyway useful to you or helped you in any way (or even if it didn't) – you can drop me an email (shanewilliamkeenan@gmail.com) about the bits you liked or didn't like, and I will read every one of them.

Printed in Great Britain
by Amazon